HAVE
HOPE

HAVE HOPE

365 Encouraging Poems, Prayers, and Meditations for Daily Inspiration

Maggie Oman Shannon

Foreword by Phil Cousineau

Conari Press

Coral Gables

Cover & Layout Design: Carmen Fortunato
Cover Illustration: Flying Sky Lanterns by Tatyana / AdobeStock
Illustrations: Seasonal tree by Miroslava Hlavacova / AdobeStock

For permission requests, please contact the publisher at:
Mango Publishing Group
2850 S Douglas Road, 2nd Floor
Coral Gables, FL 33134 USA
info@mango.bz

For special orders, quantity sales, course adoptions and corporate sales, please email the publisher at sales@mango.bz. For trade and wholesale sales, please contact Ingram Publisher Services at customer.service@ingramcontent.com or +1.800.509.4887.

Have Hope: 365 Encouraging Poems, Prayers, and Meditations for
Daily Inspiration

Library of Congress Cataloging-in-Publication number: 2021934945
ISBN: (print) 978-1-64250-599-3, (ebook) 978-1-64250-598-6
BISAC: OCC019000—BODY, MIND & SPIRIT / Inspiration &
Personal Growth

Printed in the United States of America

Dedicated with deepest gratitude
to all those who intentionally give of themselves
to provide hope for others…
may each one of us dedicate ourselves
to doing the same; may each one of us
be hope

TABLE OF CONTENTS

FOREWORD

by Phil Cousineau

Myths are stories that may have never happened, but in a mysterious way are always happening. What myths reveal are forces that are constant to the human race, threads of truth that tie together what was, what is, and what will be in the soul. The ancient Greeks believed that any time a person feels an overpowering urge or an overwhelming emotion, there lurks nearby a god or goddess. If you want to know about life on the outside, you read history or study science; if you want to understand life from the inside, you read the myths; you turn to the arts.

Hope is one such mystery, a force that defies easy definition, but is as real as rain. According to the dictionary, hope is a feeling of expectation rooted in the desire for a certain thing to *happen*, a longing for life to *change* for the better, as revealed in the common expression, to hope for the best. And yet the very idea of hope has been maligned by the cynical and the snarky for as long as it has been admired, ridiculed for being naive or, worse, dangerous.

The conundrum is as old as storytelling itself as revealed by the story of Pandora's Box. First described by the sixth-century poet Hesiod, in *Work and Days*, we learn that Zeus despised the human race and wanted to destroy it and start over. The titan Prometheus felt sorry for our distant ancestors and risked his own life to save them from extinction. Secretly, he broke into the workshop of Hephaestus, god of fire, and stole a glowing ember from Hestia's sacred hearth. Hiding the ember in a fennel stalk, he carried it to earth, which, the poet tells us, helped spark the birth of the arts and sciences and eventually civilization itself. Inevitably, Zeus was outraged and sought revenge. To punish Prometheus, Zeus chained him to a rock on a mountain peak where an eagle tortured him until he was rescued by Hercules. To punish the human race, Zeus had the twisted idea of commanding Hephaestus to create the first woman who was endowed with divine gifts from each of the Olympian gods and goddesses. The god of the forge formed her out of clay and gave her a voice. Among the gift-givers was Athena, who adorned her with beautiful garments. Aphrodite cast a spell of enchantment over her so that the first man she met would fall in love with her. Hermes graced her with insatiable curiosity and cunning. And so it was that she earned the name Pandora, which means "all-gifts" or "all endowed." However, the embittered Zeus was not done. He offered her one final bittersweet gift, a jar (later translated in the Renaissance as a box) and warned Pandora to never open it.

We all know how that turned out.

The first moment Pandora was alone with the jar, she was overcome with the very curiosity that Hermes had instilled in her, along with a desire to discover something beautiful. Longing to see what secrets were hidden within, she opened the lid. Immediately, she felt a cold wind as all manner of evil spirits escaped—disease, plague, misfortune, even death itself—and spread across the earth.

Horrified, Pandora slammed the lid back down onto the jar, leaving inside one additional spirit, who was the goddess Elpis, better known as Hope, who clung to the lip of the jar and has lurked there ever since, waiting to be released.

For the last few millennia, mythographers, scholars, artists, and theologians have puzzled over why the vengeful Zeus would include Hope among the dark gifts he locked inside the jar. Was it a cruel joke, a test? Or was he living up to his own task of being one of the gods of justice and so allowing humanity a cosmic escape valve? As with all the world's wisdom stories, it is up to each of us to decide.

Often, myths are cautionary tales, warning signals sent up from the depths of the unconscious to remind us of our darker impulses. But a wider reading of the world's wisdom traditions reveals there are also numinous tales, signs in story form, that remind us of what Lincoln called the "better angels of our nature."

Have Hope is one such "nod of the gods," the original meaning of *numinous*, which is also a marvelous synonym for *sacred*. In this collection of poems, prayers, anecdotes and exhortations, Maggie Oman Shannon has gathered a year's worth of reminders of our yearning for a better world. More than an anthology, this book provides the reader with antidotes to the cynicism (the last refuge of scoundrels) that still runs rampant about the power of hope. If savored, these passages may help the reader to reconcile the paradox about its mysterious origins, which is that hope is inextricably connected with suffering.

This uncomfortable truth is confirmed on every page of this book by way of what the author calls hope quotations and hopeful events. These selections reveal how often hope has inspired dreams of a better world—but only accomplished significant change through hope-filled actions, deeds, and movements.

To the avid reader, these passages show how *hope is a practice*. Hope is active not passive, a noun *and* a verb, a muscle that must be exercised or it withers. To come back to Pandora, hope is always there in the dark recesses of our hearts and minds but needs to be released.

While riffling through the pages of *Have Hope*, I was reminded of a consolation card I recently discovered that one of my mother's sisters, my aunt Shirley, sent to her after the death of my grandma Dora. She wrote: "Rosemary, they say a person needs just a few things to be truly happy in this world: someone to love, something to do, and something to hope for."

I like to think this loving gesture provided my mother with a cushion of consolation, a vision of hope that allowed her a moment of happiness because it reminded her that life can and must go on.

Uncannily, the card also brought to mind an aphorism I once read in the London home of the inimitable Dr. Samuel Johnson, a truism that serves as a testimony to the power of this book: "Whatever enlarges hope exalts courage."

Phil Cousineau
San Francisco, 2021

INTRODUCTION

When I was in high school, a friend commented that my room was like a line in the Dorothy Parker poem "Interior"—because I had so many "mottoes on the wall." I have always had mottoes on the wall, and in boxes of papers, journals, and computer files. And since *Have Hope* is a book idea that I've had for more than two decades, working on it gave me the opportunity to comb through my mountainous hope archives and reflect on what it means to me now, as a woman in my sixties.

My perspective on hope at this point in my life is different from when I first contemplated a book of quotations on hope; then, I was thirty-nine and single, and my first book—*Prayers for Healing*—had been out for one year. My hopes then were for my future, hopes of creating not only a family but also a new career. Almost twenty-five years later, I am married, a congregational minister, the author of nine books, including this one, and the mother of a teenager applying to college—and my hope has expanded and deepened to include not only my daughter's future, but hope for the world itself. Life on the planet today has become increasingly complex, so much so that hope can seem elusive at times—but while working on this book, I have found out how helpful (and hopeful) it can be to look at historical events and to remember again that there have been dark days before. As people throughout time have discovered, history teaches us to hope.

Therefore, for this book, I looked to my first work, *Prayers for Healing*, for formatting inspiration; in that book, I sometimes tied readings to an event in time, and I thought that could be a really interesting way to organize a book of quotations on hope: with hopeful events listed for each day. Therefore, in this book, you will find 365 events in history that inspired hope at the time when each took place, and usually beyond: advancements in culture, science, technology, and governance—things that have proven to move humankind forward. As you'll see, I also include dates that marked advances in societal equality—some of the historic firsts in the areas of politics, the arts, sports, and other achievements made by people in demographic groups other than the predominantly white male bastion that has written most views of history. I also include the birthdays of individuals who made some kind of worldwide or significant impact through their lifework.

In addition to including a hopeful event for each day, I also wanted to see if I could find relevant quotations that would include the word "hope" or some form of it. My purpose in doing this was the hope that seeing how people throughout centuries have used that word and concept could give us some interesting and varying perspectives on how to view hope.

It should be noted that throughout time, hope has been seen by some as a double-edged sword—as something that could be ephemeral and even destructive, as in "false hope" or "blind hope." But by far, I found that most people past and present laud the power of hope to change our world both individually and collectively, and agree on the very real (one might even say crucial) need for it, as it can take us through demanding times.

Through the twenty-plus years from conception to publication, I have at different times put this book on the back burner, only to bring it back up and return it to my project list—the last time was when the first African American US president, Barack Obama, who ran on the very idea of hope, was in office. This book didn't get completed until the stormy end of another president's term: Obama's successor, Donald Trump. Working on the book at that time, I realized perhaps why this book took such a long time to be born. When things are going relatively well both for us and those around us, we don't look for inspiration quite as urgently as when they're not. During the completion of this book in late 2020 and early 2021, I was gathering quotations on hope during a time in America when things were looking almost hopeless, a time when the daily news was reporting the myriad (and shocking) ways in which a US president was breaking laws and seeking to stay in power even though he had lost the presidential election of 2020—and then came January 6, 2021, a day on which the entire world watched to see if America's democracy would hold.

Living through these historical events in real time brought home more than ever before just how much we humans *need* hope. This book was produced in the midst of a global pandemic, worldwide protests about systemic racism, and the aforementioned (and previously unimaginable) political unrest in America. I became freshly reconvinced of how important it is to receive an education—how crucial it is to know about those who have come before us, to have a working knowledge of human history; because as George Santayana said, "Those who cannot remember the past are condemned to repeat it."

Of course, as history continues, so will fresh mentions of hope—such as the words spoken by our new president, Joseph R. Biden, whose inaugural address did as much as anything quoted here to illustrate our need for hope. And if by chance you have the fleeting thought that many of the entries I've chosen seem political, it is because one conclusion I have become convinced of while working on this book is just how very much hope rests on a just and free society and the ability of all of its members to be fully honored and engaged in it. In stark terms that convey the essential nature of what hope brings to every person on the planet, Barack Obama phrased it this way: "The absence of hope can rot a society from within."

It is my hope that you will find a number of dates and quotations here to stoke your own sense of hope. Through the quarter century that my first book, *Prayers for Healing*, has been in publication, I've heard of so many ways in which people have used it: as a record of the birthdays of loved ones; as the start to a meditation each day; as prompts for journaling, and more. May *Have Hope* have such personal relevance for you, too…and may *Have Hope* not only bring you hope, but help to remind you that as US Representative Alexandria Ocasio-Cortez once said, you have to *be* hope. As Joan Borysenko advises us in her poem "When Hope Comes to Visit…Open the Door," may we "Dare to hope and cast our vote for love." May we all be hope for a world that so desperately needs it.

Maggie Oman Shannon
San Francisco, California
January 2021

Will miracles never cease?

A strange sensation rose up last night while watching the news.
My muscles relaxed, warmth flooded my exhausted body,
and joy radiated a soft, sweet, nearly forgotten pleasure.
Could this be hope I marveled, yielding to deep contentment.

Then, just for a minute or two, the wondrous spell broke
and fear galloped in dressed up like a menacing Darth Vader.
"How dare you hope?" it badgered, its long bony finger
pointed in derision. "Don't let your guard down, stupid."

"I know you're just trying to protect me," I purred.
"Thanks so much for your service.
But hey, I need a break. At least for now all is well.
Don't let the door hit your backside on the way out."

Basking in delight, throwing caution to the wind
I opened my heart wantonly to possibility.
This morning I feel like a smiling Cheshire Cat
Sprawled out lithely on a greening branch.

I will bask in that feeling, slurping up the unexpected
Blessing—banking hope like precious currency
to spend when dark times close in as they do.

Hope reminds me that all things inevitably pass,
but love always remains.
For the sake of our souls, and the soul of democracy
Dare to hope and be sure to cast your vote for love today.

—Joan Borysenko, "When Hope Comes to Visit...
Open the Door"
Written November 3, 2020

WINTER

Sometimes our fate resembles a fruit tree in winter.
Who would think that those branches would turn
green again and blossom,
but we hope it, we know it.

—Johann Wolfgang von Goethe

January 1

In 1971, cigarette advertisements are banned on US television beginning on this day

Now is the time,
To climb up the mountain
And reason against habit,

Now is the time.
Now is the time,
To renew the barren soil of nature
Ruined by the winds of tyranny,
Now is the time.

Now is the time,
To commence the litany of hope,
Now is the time…

Now is the time,
To give me roses, not to keep them
For my grave to come,
Give them to me while my heart beats,
Give them today
While my heart yearns for jubilee,
Now is the time…

—Mzwakhe Mbuli

January 2

*In 1968, Dr. Christian Barnard performs the first successful
heart transplant*

> We always kept in our hearts the most noble, beautiful
> feeling that sets human beings apart: Hope.
>
> —Manel Loureiro

January 3

*In 1993, US President George Bush and Russian President
Boris Yeltsin sign the START-II (Strategic Arms Reduction
Talks) Treaty, eliminating about two-thirds of each country's
munitions stockpile*

> No problem of human making is too great to be overcome
> by human ingenuity, human energy, and the untiring hope
> of the human spirit.
>
> —George H.W. Bush

January 4

*In 1809, Louis Braille—blinded as a boy and inventor of a
reading system for the blind—is born in France*

> It is because of hope that you suffer. It is through hope that
> you'll change things.
>
> —Maxime Legace

January 5

In 1905, the National Association of the Audubon Society incorporates

> "Hope" is the thing with
> feathers—
> That perches in the soul—
> And sings the tune without the words—
> And never stops—at all—
>
> —Emily Dickinson

January 6

In 2021, a seditious mob of Trump supporters storms the US Capitol seeking to overturn election results. Despite this, the US Congress reconvenes five hours later and certifies the election of President-Elect Joe Biden

> It was the best of times, it was the worst of times, it was the age of wisdom, it was the age of foolishness, it was the epoch of belief, it was the epoch of incredulity, it was the season of light, it was the season of darkness, it was the spring of hope, it was the winter of despair.
>
> —Charles Dickens

January 7

In 1927, the Harlem Globetrotters play their first game

Don't ever give up hope until the very last moment. If you give up, the game is already over.

—*Takehiko Inoue in Slam Dunk, Tome 1*

January 8

In 1790, US President George Washington delivers the first State of the Union Address

Three things prompt men to a regular discharge of their duty in time of action: natural bravery, hope of reward, and fear of punishment.

—George Washington

January 9

In 1859, Carrie Lane Chapman, founder of the National League of Women Voters, is born

The vote is a power, a weapon of offense and defense, a prayer. Understand what it means and what it can do for your country. Use it intelligently, conscientiously, prayerfully. No soldier in the great suffrage army has labored and suffered to get a "place" for you. Their motive has been the hope that women would aim higher than their own selfish ambitions, that they would serve the common good.

—Carrie Lane Chapman

January 10

In 1967, the Public Broadcasting System (PBS), a national educational television organization, begins as a seventy-station network

> As for the passions and studies of the mind: avoid envy; anxious fears; anger fretting inwards; joys and exhilarations in excess; sadness not communicated. Entertain hopes; mirth rather than joy; variety of delights, rather than surfeit of them; wonder and admiration, and therefore novelties; studies that fill the mind with splendid and illustrious objects, as histories, fables, and contemplations of nature.
>
> —Francis Bacon

January 11

In 1989, 140 nations agree to ban chemical weapons, including poison gas

> Man himself has become our greatest hazard and our only hope.
>
> —John Steinbeck

January 12

In 1932, Hattie W. Caraway becomes the first woman elected to the US Senate

Hope is not something that you have. Hope is something that you create, with your actions. Hope is contagious. Other people start acting in a way that has more hope.

—US Representative Alexandria Ocasio-Cortez

January 13

In 1990, L. Douglas Wilder of Virginia becomes the first African American governor in the United States

Hope is like the sun, which, as we journey toward it, casts the shadow of our burden behind us.

—Samuel Smiles

January 14

In 1875, philosopher-physician and Nobel Peace Prize winner Albert Schweitzer is born in Germany

To the question whether I am a pessimist or an optimist, I answer that my knowledge is pessimistic, but my willing and hoping are optimistic.

—Albert Schweitzer

January 15

In 1697, the citizens of Massachusetts spend a day of fasting and repentance for their roles in the 1692 Salem witch trials. The judge who presided over many of the trials publishes a confession acknowledging his own "blame and shame."

We share responsibility for creating the external world by projecting either a spirit of light or a spirit of shadow on that which is "other" than us. Either a spirit of hope or a spirit of despair. Either an inner confidence in wholeness and integration or an inner terror about life being diseased and ultimately terminal. We have a choice about what we are going to project, and in that choice, we help create the world that is.

—Parker J. Palmer

January 16

In 1992, the twelve-year civil war in El Salvador ends, having claimed over 75,000 lives

The past is dead; let it bury its dead, its hopes and its aspirations; before you lies the future—a future full of golden promise.

—Jefferson Davis

January 17

In 1964, American attorney, author, and First Lady Michelle Obama is born

Don't ever make decisions based on fear. Make decisions based on hope and possibility. Make decisions based on what should happen, not what shouldn't.

—Michelle Obama

January 18

In 1966, Robert Clifton Weaver is sworn in as the first African American Cabinet member in US history

> Most [Black] Americans still are not only outside the mainstream of our society but see no hope of entering it.... And the quality and nature of future [Black] leadership depends upon how effective those leaders who relate to the total society can be in satisfying the yearnings for human dignity which reside in the hearts of all Americans.
>
> —Robert C. Weaver, in a 1963 speech

January 19

In 1981, the US and Iran sign an agreement calling for the release of fifty-two Americans held hostage for more than fourteen months

> Just as despair can come to one only from other human beings, hope, too, can be given to one only by other human beings.
>
> —Elie Wiesel

January 20

In 2021, Kamala Harris is sworn in as the first female, first African American, and first Asian American vice president of the United States

You marched and organized for equality and justice; for our lives, and for our planet. And then you voted. You delivered a clear message. You chose hope, unity, decency, science, and yes, truth.

—Kamala Harris

January 21

In 1799, Edward Jenner's smallpox vaccine is introduced

Vaccines are the hope of the future.

—Dr. Anthony Fauci

January 22

In 1952, the first commercial jet plane is put into service

Fly high with strong hopes.

—Amirtha Keerthi

January 23

In 1849, Elizabeth Blackwell becomes the first woman doctor in the United States

[M]y hope rises when I find that the inner heart of a human being may remain pure, notwithstanding some corruption of the outer coverings.

—Elizabeth Blackwell

January 24

In 1962, Jackie Robinson becomes the first Black player elected to the Baseball Hall of Fame

> Kids are our future, and we hope baseball has given them some idea of what it is to live together and how we can get along, whether you be Black or white.
>
> —Larry Doby

January 25

In 2021, Janet Yellen is confirmed as the first American female Secretary of the Treasury

> Hope has two beautiful daughters; their names are Anger and Courage; Anger at the way things are, and Courage to see that they do not remain as they are.
>
> —St. Augustine of Hippo

January 26

In 1904, Irish statesman and Amnesty International cofounder Sean MacBride is born

> Hope is useless unless it is tied to action. Action is destructive unless it is tied to hope.
>
> —Anonymous

January 27

In 1973, the Vietnam Peace Accords are signed in Paris, officially ending the Vietnam War

> What kind of peace do we seek? Not a Pax Americana enforced on the world by American weapons of war. Not the peace of the grave or the security of the slave. I am talking about genuine peace, the kind of peace that makes life on earth worth living, the kind that enables men and nations to grow and to hope and to build a better life for their children…not merely peace in our time, but peace for all time.
>
> —John F. Kennedy

January 28

In 1902, the Carnegie Institution is founded in Washington, DC, to "encourage investigation, research, and discovery [and] show the application of knowledge to the improvement of mankind"

> The past is a source of knowledge, and the future is a source of hope. Love of the past implies faith in the future.
>
> —Stephen Ambrose

January 29

In 1978, Sweden becomes the first country to outlaw aerosol sprays due to the harmful effects on the ozone layer

To cherish what remains of the Earth and to foster its renewal is our only legitimate hope of survival.

—Wendell Berry

January 30

In 1882, Franklin D. Roosevelt, the thirty-second US president, is born

> We have always held to the hope, the belief, the conviction that there is a better life, a better world, beyond the horizon.

—Franklin D. Roosevelt

January 31

In 1865, Congress passes the Thirteenth Amendment, abolishing slavery in America

> Home was not a perfect place. But it was the only home they had and they could hope to make it better.

—Dean Koontz

February 1

In 1884, the Oxford English Dictionary is first published

> Literacy is a bridge from misery to hope. It is a tool for daily life in modern society. It is a bulwark against poverty and a building block of development, an essential complement to

investments in roads, dams, clinics, and factories. Literacy is a platform for democratization and a vehicle for the promotion of cultural and national identity. Especially for girls and women, it is an agent of family health and nutrition. For everyone, everywhere, literacy is, along with education in general, a basic human right…. Literacy is, finally, the road to human progress and the means through which every man, woman, and child can realize his or her full potential.

—Kofi Annan

February 2

In 1990, South African President F.W. de Klerk lifts ban on the African National Congress and promises to free Nelson Mandela

None who have always been free can understand the terrible fascinating power of the hope of freedom to those who are not free.

—Pearl S. Buck

February 3

In 1919, the League of Nations holds its first meeting in Paris

It was our duty to see to it that every decision we took part in contributed, so far as we were able to influence it, to quiet the fears and realize the hopes of the peoples who had been living in that shadow, the nations that had come by our assistance to their freedom. It was our duty to do everything that it was within our power to do to make the triumph of freedom and of right a lasting triumph in the assurance of which men might everywhere live without fear.

—Woodrow Wilson

February 4

In 1938, the play Our Town *by Thornton Wilder opens on Broadway*

Hope, like faith, is nothing if it is not courageous; it is nothing if it is not ridiculous.

—Thornton Wilder

February 5

In 1917, Mexico's current constitution is adopted

Hope dies last of all.

—Mexican proverb

February 6

In 2000, Foreign Minister Tarja Halonen becomes the first woman elected president of Finland

A leader is a dealer in hope.

—Napoleon Bonaparte

February 7

In 1812, English author Charles Dickens is born

"Hope to the last!" said Newman, clapping him on the back. "Always hope; that's a dear boy. Never leave off hoping; it don't answer. Do you mind me, Nick? It don't answer. Don't leave a stone unturned. It's always something, to know you've done the most you could. But don't leave off hoping, or it's of no use doing anything. Hope, hope, to the last!"

—Charles Dickens, *Nicholas Nickleby*

February 8

In 1883, Louis Waterman begins experimentation on his way to inventing the fountain pen

I am but a pen, and one day my ink will run out. I only hope I have created something beautiful in the meantime.

—Anonymous

February 9

In 1944, American author Alice Walker is born

It has become a common feeling, I believe, as we have watched our heroes falling over the years, that our own small stone of activism, which might not seem to measure up to the rugged boulders of heroism we have so admired, is a paltry offering toward the building of an edifice of hope. Many who believe this choose to withhold their offerings out of shame. This is the tragedy of the world. For we can do nothing substantial toward changing our course on the planet...without rousing ourselves, individual by individual, and bringing our small, imperfect stones to the pile.

—Alice Walker

February 10

In 1989, Ron Brown is elected chairman of the Democratic Party, the first African American elected chairman of a major political party

Hope is essential to any political struggle for radical change when the overall social climate promotes disillusionment and despair.

—bell hooks

February 11

In 1752, the first hospital in America opens in Pennsylvania

Hope and reality lie in inverse proportions, inside the walls of a hospital...

—Jodi Picoult

February 12

In 1809, Abraham Lincoln, the sixteenth US president, is born

I now leave, not knowing when or whether ever I may return, with a task before me greater than that which rested upon Washington. Without the assistance of that Divine Being who ever attended him, I cannot succeed. With that assistance I cannot fail. Trusting in Him who can go with me, and remain with you, and be everywhere for good, let us confidently hope that all will yet be well.

—Abraham Lincoln, Farewell Address at Springfield,
February 11, 1861

February 13

In 1635, the Boston Latin School—the first public school in the United States—is founded

Education breeds confidence. Confidence breeds hope. Hope breeds peace.

—Confucius

February 14

*In 1818, African American abolitionist Frederick
Douglass is born*

> The thought of only being a creature of the present and
> past was troubling. I longed for a future too, with hope in it.
> The desire to be free awakened my determination to act, to
> think, and to speak.
>
> —Frederick Douglass

February 15

*In 1820, American women's rights activist Susan B.
Anthony is born*

> There is no history about which there is so much ignorance
> as this great movement for the establishment of equal
> political rights for women. I hope the twentieth century will
> see the triumph of our cause.
>
> —Susan B. Anthony

February 16

*In 1968, the first 911 emergency service in the United States goes
into effect*

> Always remember that it's your voice in the darkness that
> gives hope to those who really need it.
>
> —Anonymous EMT/Paramedic

February 17

In 1911, Cadillac introduces the first automobile with an electric self-starter instead of a hand crank

Hope is one of the principal springs that keep mankind in motion.

—Thomas Fuller

February 18

In 1931, American author Toni Morrison is born

I am charmed by the idea that there is an activity known as work and another as play, although even in grade school, the distinction eluded me. I remember how full of hope I was sitting in first-period home room listening to the teacher divide up our activities into purposeful sections. I got a grip on her process, at last, by picturing it in the following way: A cow stands in clover. When she is milked, that is her work; when she is merely eating, that is her play. But the problem lay, then as now, in the realization that in any case, she is standing in clover. Not a handsome or elegant analogy, but it approximates for me the habit of reading—standing in a world of clover, the eating of which is occasionally utilitarian, usually nourishing, because that's what one does.

—Toni Morrison

February 19

In 1963, The Feminine Mystique *by Betty Friedan is published*

In almost every professional field, in business and in the arts and sciences, women are still treated as second-class citizens. It would be a great service to tell girls who plan to work in society to expect this subtle, uncomfortable discrimination—tell them not to be quiet and hope it will go away, but fight it. A girl should not expect special privileges because of her sex, but neither should she "adjust" to prejudice and discrimination.

—Betty Friedan

February 20

In 1792, the US Postal Service is created

Strange as it may seem, I still hope for the best, even though the best, like an interesting piece of mail, so rarely arrives, and even when it does, it can be lost so easily.

—Lemony Snicket in *The Beatrice Letters*

February 21

In 1885, the Washington Monument is officially dedicated in Washington, DC

Hope is patience with a lamp lit.

—Tertullian

February 22

In 1980, the US ice hockey team defeats the Soviet Union to win the Olympic gold medal in the "Miracle on Ice"

Where there is hope, there is faith. Where there is faith, miracles happen.

—Anonymous

February 23

In 1455, German Johannes Gutenberg prints the first Bible

God is our hope and strength,
a very present hope in trouble.

—Psalms 46:1

February 24

In 1970, National Public Radio begins broadcasting in the United States

Our blessed radio. It gives us eyes and ears out into the world. We listen to the German station only for good music. And we listen to the BBC for hope.

—Anne Frank

February 25

In 1870, Hiram Rhodes Revels becomes the first African American to serve in the United States Senate

> If the nation should take a step for the encouragement of this prejudice against the colored race, can they have any ground upon which to predicate a hope that Heaven will smile upon them and prosper them? …Sir, this prejudice should be resisted.
>
> —Hiram Rhodes Revels

February 26

In 1991, the first Internet browser, WorldWideWeb, is introduced (later renamed Nexus)

> I hope we will use the Net to cross barriers and connect cultures.
>
> —Tim Berners-Lee

February 27

In 1922, the US Supreme Court upholds the Nineteenth Amendment, which guarantees women the right to vote

> Hope just means another world might be possible, not promised, not guaranteed. Hope calls for action; action is impossible without hope.
>
> —Rebecca Solnit

February 28

In 1933, Frances Perkins becomes the first female to serve in the United States Senate

> To one who believes that really good industrial conditions are the hope for a machine civilization, nothing is more heartening than to watch conference methods and education replacing police methods.
>
> —Frances Perkins

February 29 (Leap Year)

In 1940, Hattie McDaniel becomes the first African American woman to win an Oscar (for Gone with the Wind*)*

> Academy of Motion Picture Arts and Sciences, fellow members of the motion picture industry and honored guests: This is one of the happiest moments of my life, and I want to thank each one of you who had a part in selecting me for one of their awards for your kindness. It has made me feel very, very humble; and I shall always hold it as a beacon for anything that I may be able to do in the future. I sincerely hope I shall always be a credit to my race and to the motion picture industry. My heart is too full to tell you just how I feel, and may I say thank you and God bless you.
>
> —Hattie McDaniel's Academy Award acceptance speech

March 1

In 1872, Yellowstone, the first US National Park, is established

Hope is a force of nature. Don't let anyone tell
you different.

—Jim Butcher

March 2

In 1917, citizens of Puerto Rico are granted US citizenship

Mas larga(o) que la esperanza de un pobre.
Say this [Puerto Rican] phrase, which translates to "longer
than the hope of a poor man," when you can't see an end to
something. The phrase comes from the idea that someone
with a low income always has hope that the situation will
get better in the long run.

—Mariela Santos

March 3

In 1849, the US Department of the Interior is established

In God's wildness lies the hope of the world—the great
fresh unblighted, unredeemed wilderness. The galling
harness of civilization drops off, and wounds heal ere we
are aware.

—John Muir

March 4

In 1917, Jeannette Rankin becomes the first female member of the US House of Representatives

Politics hates a vacuum. If it isn't filled with hope, someone will fill it with fear.

—Naomi Klein

March 5

In 1991, Iraq releases all Gulf War prisoners

When you have lost hope, you have lost everything. And when you think all is lost, when all is dire and bleak, there is always hope.

—Pittacus Lore

March 6

In 1475, Renaissance artist Michelangelo Buonarroti is born

Many believe—and I believe—that I have been designated for this work by God. In spite of my old age, I do not want to give it up; I work out of love for God and I put all my hope in Him.

—Michelangelo

March 7

In 1969, Golda Meir is elected the first female prime minister of Israel

> There is only one thing I hope to see before I die, and that is that my people should not need expressions of sympathy anymore.
>
> —Golda Meir

March 8

In 1841, US Supreme Court Justice Oliver Wendell Holmes Jr. is born

> Beware how you take away hope from another human being.
>
> —Oliver Wendell Holmes Jr.

March 9

In 1841, a judge rules that captured Africans who seized the slave-trading ship La Amistad were enslaved illegally

> We hope the Lord will love you very much & take you up to heaven when you die. We pray for all the good people who make us free. Wicked people want to make us slaves but the great God who has made all things raise up friends

for Mendi people he give us Mr. Adams the he may make me free & all Mendi people free…

—From a letter to John Quincy Adams from the Amistad captives, who were freed after the Supreme Court ruled in their favor

March 10

In 1776, Common Sense *by Thomas Paine is published, inspiring American patriots to declare independence from Great Britain*

I believe in one God and no more, and I hope for happiness beyond this life. I believe in the equality of man; and I believe that religious duties consist in doing justice, loving mercy, and endeavoring to make our fellow creatures happy.

—Thomas Paine

March 11

In 1918, the Save the Redwoods League is founded

Look at a tree when you lose hope. First it was a seed below the ground, and only with patience it was able to touch the sky above.

—Roxana Jones

March 12

In 1930, Gandhi begins his two-hundred-mile march to the sea to defy British rule over India

> When every hope is gone, "when helpers fail and comforts flee," I find that help arrives somehow, from I know not where. Supplication, worship, [and] prayer are no superstition; they are acts more real than the acts of eating, drinking, sitting, or walking. It is no exaggeration to say that they alone are real, all else is unreal.
>
> —Mahatma Gandhi

March 13

In 1901, US multimillionaire Andrew Carnegie announces he is retiring to spend the rest of his life giving away his fortune

> If you want to be happy, set a goal that commands your thoughts, liberates your energy, and inspires your hopes.
>
> —Andrew Carnegie

March 14

In 1879, Nobel Prize-winning physicist Albert Einstein is born in Germany

> Learn from yesterday, live for today, hope for tomorrow. The important thing is not to stop questioning.
>
> —Attributed to Albert Einstein

March 15

In 1933, US Supreme Court Justice Ruth Bader Ginsberg is born

Dissents speak to a future age. It's not simply to say, "My colleagues are wrong, and I would do it this way." But the greatest dissents do become court opinions, and gradually, over time their views become the dominant view. So that's the dissenter's hope: that they are writing not for today, but for tomorrow.

—Ruth Bader Ginsberg

March 16

In 1912, Mrs. William Howard Taft plants the first cherry tree in Washington, DC

As long as the sun smiles above us, our hopes will always blossom.

—Atalay Aydin

March 17

In 1992, Black people obtain equal rights under the law in South Africa

The task at hand will not be easy, but you have mandated us to change South Africa from a land in which the majority lived with little hope to one in which they can live and work with dignity, with a sense of self-esteem and confidence in the future.

—Nelson Mandela, from his 1994 inauguration speech

March 18

In 1662, Paris establishes the first public transportation service

You do not need to know precisely what is happening or exactly where it is all going. What you need is to recognize the possibilities and challenges offered by the present moment, and to embrace them with courage, faith, and hope.

—Thomas Merton

March 19

In 1891, US Supreme Court Justice Earl Warren is born

It is from numberless diverse acts of courage and belief that human history is shaped. Each time a man stands up for an ideal, or acts to improve the lot of others, or strikes out against injustice, he sends forth a tiny ripple of hope; and crossing each other from a million different centers of energy and daring, those ripples build a current that can sweep down the mightiest walls of oppression and resistance.

—Robert F. Kennedy

SPRING

*In the springtime, hope blooms
in even the loneliest
forgotten meadow.*

—Angie Weiland-Crosby

March 20

In 1928, Fred Rogers, minister and creator of Mister Rogers' Neighborhood, *is born*

> My hope and wish is that one day, formal education will pay attention to what I call "education of the heart." Just as we take for granted the need to acquire proficiency in the basic academic subjects, I am hopeful that a time will come when we can take it for granted that children will learn as part of the curriculum the indispensability of inner values: love, compassion, justice, and forgiveness.
>
> —The Dalai Lama

March 21

In 1965, Rev. Martin Luther King and more than three thousand civil rights demonstrators begin a march from Selma to Montgomery, Alabama

> If you lose hope, somehow you lose the vitality that keeps moving, you lose that courage to be, that quality that helps you go on in spite of it all. And so today, I still have a dream.
>
> —Dr. Martin Luther King Jr.

March 22

In 1873, Spain abolishes slavery

> Free labor has the inspiration of hope; pure slavery
> has no hope.
>
> —Abraham Lincoln

March 23

In 1903, the Wright Brothers patent the airplane

> What we hope ever to do with ease, we must first learn to
> do with diligence.
>
> —Samuel Johnson

March 24

In 1837, Canada gives Black men the right to vote

> He who does not hope to win has already lost.
>
> —Jose Joaquin de Olmedo

March 25

In 1934, women's rights activist Gloria Steinem is born

> After all, hope is a form of planning. If our hopes weren't
> already real within us, we couldn't even hope them.
>
> —Gloria Steinem

March 26

In 1953, Dr. Jonas Salk announces a new polio vaccine

Hope lies in dreams, in imagination, and in the courage of those who dare to make dreams into reality.

—Jonas Salk, MD

March 27

In 1948, days after being released from prison, Billie Holiday plays in front of a sold-out crowd at Carnegie Hall

It's been hard to hold on to hope this year.… I've been sad and turned to the music that taught me how to find the beauty in pain. I've been playing Billie Holiday songs across America with my musician's voice reaching back to join hers.…

This music has made me new friends, told me new stories, brought back things I thought I'd lost a long time ago. It's brought me home. After all the years, all the travels, all the music, I've understood the lesson I've learned from Lady Day: that the magic in making music, as in living life, is to forget about all the definitions and rules you ever learned, to lean back against the launchpad of your history and your experience, your losses and heartaches and joys, to look out into the future and to make something that is completely your own.

—Lara Downes

March 28

In 1990, US President George H.W. Bush posthumously awards Olympics star Jesse Owens the Congressional Gold Medal

An athlete cannot run with money in his pockets. He must run with hope in his heart and dreams in his head.

—Emil Zatopek

March 29

In 1973, the last American soldiers leave Vietnam

Hope is important because it can make the present moment less difficult to bear. If we believe that tomorrow will be better, we can bear a hardship today.

—Thich Nhat Hanh

March 30

In 1932, Amelia Earhart becomes the first woman to make a solo flight across the Atlantic Ocean

The morning sky is hope
to paint a dream
in the early light...

—Junti

March 31

In 1927, American labor leader and civil rights activist Cesar Chavez is born

I have met many, many farm workers and friends who love justice and who are willing to sacrifice for what is right. They have a quality about them that reminds me of the beatitudes. They are living examples that Jesus' promise is true: They have been hungry and thirsty for righteousness, and they have been satisfied. They are determined, patient people who believe in life and who give strength to others. They have given me more love and hope and strength than they will ever know.

—Cesar Chavez

April 1

In 1946, Weight Watchers is formed

Tomorrow is the most important thing in life. Comes into us at midnight very clean. It's perfect when it arrives and it puts itself in our hands. It hopes we've learned something from yesterday.

—John Wayne

April 2

In 2013, the UN General Assembly approves the first Arms Trade Treaty

> The United Nations is the best hope to spare humanity from the barbarity of war, from the senseless death, destruction, and dislocation it brings about.
>
> —Alfred-Maurice de Zayas

April 3

In 1860, the Pony Express mail service begins

> To communicate the truths of history is an act of hope for the future.
>
> —Daisaku Ikeda

April 4

In 1802, Dorothea Dix, American advocate for the indigent mentally ill, is born

> While we diminish the stimulant of *fear*, we must increase to prisoners the incitements of *hope*; in proportion as we extinguish the *terrors* of the law, we should awaken and strengthen the *control* of the *conscience*.
>
> —Dorothea Dix

April 5

In 1856, African American leader, educator, and presidential advisor Booker T. Washington is born

You go to school, you study about the Germans and the French, but not about your own race. I hope the time will come when you study Black history too.

—Booker T. Washington

April 6

In 1896, the first modern Olympic Games begin in Athens, Greece

Only the strongest shoulders can carry the hopes of a nation.

—Katie Taylor, Irish Olympic gold medalist (2012)

April 7

In 1983, specialists Story Musgrave and Don Peterson make the first spacewalk from the Space Shuttle

With so much conflict in the world, space exploration can be a beacon of hope.

—Anne McClain

April 8

In 563 BC, Buddha is born

> There is a saying in Tibetan, "Tragedy should be utilized as a source of strength." No matter what sort of difficulties, how painful experience is, if we lose our hope, that's our real disaster.
>
> —The Dalai Lama

April 9

In 1939, African American contralto Marian Anderson sings at the Lincoln Memorial after being refused the right to sing at Constitution Hall

> I do not have to tell you that I dearly love the Negro spirituals. They are the unburdenings of the sorrows of an entire race, which, finding scant happiness on Earth, turns to the future for its joys.... They are my own music. But it is not for that reason that I love to sing them. I love them because they are truly spiritual in quality; they give forth the aura of faith, simplicity, humility, and hope.
>
> —Marian Anderson

April 10

In 1866, the American Society for the Prevention of Cruelty to Animals (ASPCA) is created

Last night I stood outside the tent and watched the lake and the sky, and slowly I was overcome by some pathetic yearning and simultaneously with a terrible sense of loss and sorrow. It was as if something had died or had been permanently lost—not just to me but to everyone, forever. And I thought of the animals here and the birds and the fish—even of the insects and of the men and women who were once here, simply, as a natural part of this place—and not just here, but everywhere. And I knew that we had made a separation from them all and from all of this and that we could never, never get it back. All we could do—or hope to do—was to save the little bits of it left. And I thought of all the birds asleep somewhere behind me in their tree—in their forest—and I thought: We were meant to be one thing—not separate, partitioned. We are no better and no worse—no larger and no smaller in worth—than any other creature who walks or crawls or flies or swims. We are merely different.

I saw then what I'd come to find and had found: my identity in common with this planet and perhaps, for all I know, with this universe. And I knew then what my prayer is and will remain: Make peace with nature, first; make peace with nature…now.

—Timothy Findley

April 11

In 1945, during WWII, American soldiers liberate the Nazi concentration camp in Buchenwald, Germany

Where there's hope, there's life. It fills us with fresh courage and makes us strong again.

—Anne Frank

April 12

In 1961, Russian Yuri Gagarin becomes the first man in space and the first to orbit the earth

The planet's hope and salvation lie in the adoption of revolutionary new knowledge being revealed at the frontiers of science.

—Bruce H. Lipton

April 13

In 1743, Thomas Jefferson, the third US president, is born

My theory has always been that if we are to dream, the flatteries of hope are as cheap, and pleasanter, than the gloom of despair.

—Thomas Jefferson

April 14

In 1775, the first abolitionist society in the United States is organized, with Benjamin Franklin as president

I pray for hope for those who feel none.
I pray for those in despair
to be lifted by the power of love.
I pray we all can be a part
of making this prayer come true.

—Steve Williamson

April 15

In 1923, insulin becomes generally available to people suffering with diabetes

He who has health, has hope; and he who has hope has everything.

—Thomas Carlyle

April 16

*In 1972, two Giant Pandas arrive in the United States from
China, symbolizing cross-cultural collaboration*

> "Don't hope for a life without problems," the panda said.
> "There's no such thing. Instead, hope for a life full of
> good problems."
>
> —Mark Manson

April 17

In 1970, Apollo 13 *returns safely to Earth after an
onboard accident*

> You will be secure, because there is hope; you will look
> about you and take your rest in safety.
>
> —Job 11:18–19

April 18

In 1950, the first transatlantic jet passenger trip is completed

> Hope is the destination that we seek.
> Love is the road that leads to hope.
> Courage is the motor that drives us.
> We travel out of darkness into faith.
>
> —Dean Koontz

April 19

In 1977, Alex Haley receives a special Pulitzer Prize for his book Roots

I wasn't going to be one of those people who died wondering *what if?*—I would keep putting my dreams to the test, even though it meant living with uncertainty and fear of failure. This is the shadowland of hope, and anyone with a dream must learn to live there.

—Alex Haley

April 20

In 1902, French scientists Marie and Pierre Curie isolate the radioactive element radium

You cannot hope to build a better world without improving the individuals. To that end, each of us must work for his own improvement, and at the same time share a general responsibility for all humanity, our particular duty being to aid those to whom we think we can be most useful.

—Marie Curie

April 21

In 753 BC, according to legend, Rome is founded

Hope is the pillar that holds up the world. Hope is the dream of a waking man.

—Ancient Roman author Pliny the Elder

April 22

In 1970, the first Earth Day is observed

> Remain faithful to the earth, my brothers and sisters, with the power of your virtue. Let your gift-giving love and your knowledge serve the meaning of the earth. Thus I beg and beseech you. Do not let them fly away from earthly things and beat with their wings against eternal walls. Alas, there has always been so much virtue that has flown away. Lead back to the earth the virtue that flew away…back to the body, back to life, that it may give the earth a meaning… Verily, the earth shall yet become a site of recovery. And even now a new fragrance surrounds it, bringing salvation—and a new hope.
>
> —Friedrich Nietzsche

April 23

In 1564, English playwright William Shakespeare is born

> True hope is swift and flies with swallow's wings. Kings it makes gods, and meaner creatures kings.
>
> —William Shakespeare

April 24

In 1981, the IBM personal computer is introduced

> Don't feel as if the key to successful computing is only
> in your hands. What's in your hands, I think and hope, is
> intelligence: the ability to see the machine as more than
> when you were first led up to it, that you can make it more.
>
> —Alan J. Perlis

April 25

*In 1993, a gay-rights demonstration in Washington, DC, draws
hundreds of thousands of participants*

> I know you can't live on hope alone; but without hope, life
> is not worth living. So you, and you and you: You got to
> give them hope; you got to give them hope.
>
> —Harvey Milk

April 26

*In 1785, American ornithologist and painter John James
Audubon is born*

> But hopes are shy birds flying at a great distance, seldom
> reached by the best of guns.
>
> —John James Audubon

April 27

In 2006 in Manhattan, construction begins on Freedom Tower, the replacement to the World Trade Center

> A lesson for all of us is that for every loss, there is victory, for every sadness, there is joy, and when you think you've lost everything, there is hope.
>
> —Geraldine Solon

April 28

In 1932, a vaccine for yellow fever is announced

> The miserable have no other medicine but only hope.
>
> —William Shakespeare

April 29

In 1913, Swedish-born US inventor Gideon Sundback patents the zipper in its modern form

> Hope, even more than necessity, is the mother of invention.
>
> —Jonathan Sacks

April 30

In 1789, George Washington takes office as the first president of the United States

I hope I shall possess firmness and virtue enough to maintain what I consider the most enviable of all titles, the character of an honest man.

—George Washington

May 1

In 1931, the Empire State Building in Manhattan is opened, the tallest building in the world at that time

Everything's got a purpose, really—you just have to look for it.
Cats are good at keeping old dogs alive.
Loss helps you reach for gain.
Death helps you celebrate life.
War helps you work for peace.
A flood makes you glad you're still standing.
And a tall boy can stop the wind so a candle of hope can burn bright.

—Joan Bauer, *Stand Tall*

May 2

In 1903, American pediatrician and bestselling author of Baby and Child Care *Benjamin Spock is born*

Our greatest hope is to bring up children inspired by their opportunities for being helpful and loving.

—Dr. Benjamin Spock

May 3

In 1979, Margaret Thatcher becomes the first woman elected Prime Minister of Great Britain

> Where there is discord, may we bring harmony. Where there is error, may we bring truth. Where there is doubt, may we bring faith. And where there is despair, may we bring hope.
>
> > —Margaret Thatcher, after the Peace Prayer of St. Francis of Assisi, on the occasion of her election as prime minister

May 4

In 1796, American politician and educational reformer Horace Mann is born

> Under the sublime law of progress, the present outgrows the past. The great heart of humanity is heaving with the hopes of a brighter day. All the higher instincts of our nature prophesy its approach; and the best intellects of the race are struggling to turn that prophecy into fulfilment.
>
> > —Horace Mann

May 5

In 1961, Alan Shepard becomes the first American in space

The last man on the moon, Gene Cernan, had paused for a final look at the black beauty of the world about him. He had a message to send home before departing. "As I take these last steps from the surface for some time in the future to come, I'd just like to record that America's challenge of today has forged man's destiny of tomorrow. And as we leave the moon and Taurus-Littrow, we leave as we came, and, God willing, we shall return, with peace and hope for all mankind."

—Alan Shepard, in his book *Moon Shot*

May 6

In 1954, England's Roger Bannister becomes the first person to run a mile in under four minutes

Do not hope to cross the finish line, expect it.

—Michael D'Aulerio

May 7

In 1945, Germany signs an unconditional surrender, ending World War II in Europe

Lead us from death to life, from falsehood to truth.
Lead us from despair to hope, from fear to trust.
Let peace fill our hearts, our world, our universe.
Let us dream together, pray together, work together,
to build one world
of peace and justice for all.

—Anonymous

May 8

In 1926, British naturalist and environmentalist David Attenborough is born

I spend a lot of time wringing my hands and saying how dreadful it is that this forest has been obliterated and that sea has been polluted and whatever. But there are signs of hope…. There has been a worldwide shift, I think, among people in general about the concern there should be for the natural world. I am encouraged more than I have been for some time.

—David Attenborough

May 9

In 1994, Nelson Mandela is chosen to be the first Black president of South Africa

> I never lost hope that this great transformation would occur, not only because of the great heroes I have already cited, but because of the courage of the ordinary men and women of my country. I always knew that deep down in every human heart, there is mercy and generosity.... Man's goodness is a flame that can be hidden but never extinguished.

> —Nelson Mandela

May 10

In 1869, the meeting of the Central Pacific and Union Pacific railroads in Promontory, Utah—creating the first transcontinental railroad in the United States—is celebrated

> Do not let the train of life stop at the despair station—always keep the ticket of hope!

> —Anonymous

May 11

In 1989, Kenya announces a worldwide ban on ivory to preserve its elephant herds

> The Buddhists have a story about blind men trying to describe an elephant by feeling its various parts, and each describes the elephant according to the part he touched. That is the way we can hope to know God.
>
> —Kent Nerburn

May 12

In 1820, British social reformer and founder of modern nursing Florence Nightingale is born

> A nurse will always give us hope, an angel with a stethoscope.
>
> —Terri Guillemets

May 13

In 1767, Wolfgang Amadeus Mozart's first opera Apollo et Hyacinthus, *written when he was eleven years old, premieres in Salzburg, Austria*

> I know life is hard, but we can always find hope in music and wash away our tears.
>
> —Miyavi

May 14

In 1787, delegates begin meeting in Philadelphia to discuss and write a new American constitution

Administered by some of the most eminent men who contributed to its [the US Constitution's] formation… it has not disappointed the hopes and aspirations of those illustrious benefactors of their age and nation. It has promoted the lasting welfare of that country so dear to us all; it has to an extent far beyond the ordinary lot of humanity secured the freedom and happiness of this people. We now receive it as a precious inheritance from those to whom we are indebted for its establishment, doubly bound by the examples which they have left us and by the blessings which we have enjoyed as the fruits of their labors to transmit the same unimpaired to the succeeding generation.

—John Quincy Adams

May 15

In 1918, the US Post Office began the world's first regular airmail service, between Washington, DC, and New York City

Do not spoil what you have by desiring what you have not; remember that what you now have was once among the things you only hoped for.

—Epicurus

May 16

In 1804, educator and founder of the US kindergarten system Elizabeth Palmer Peabody is born

Children are the world's most valuable resource and its best hope for the future.

—John F. Kennedy

May 17

In 1954, the US Supreme Court unanimously rules for school integration

Hope. It's like a drop of honey, a field of tulips blooming in the springtime. It's a fresh rain, a whispered promise, a cloudless sky, the perfect punctuation mark at the end of a sentence. And it's the only thing in the world keeping me afloat.

—Tahereh Mafi

May 18

In 1860, Abraham Lincoln is nominated at the National Republican Convention as its presidential nominee

My dream is of a place and a time where America will once again be seen as the last best hope of earth.

—Abraham Lincoln

May 19

In 1857, Americans William Francis Channing and Moses G. Farmer patent the electric fire alarm

> The best bridge between despair and hope is a good night's sleep.
>
> —E. Joseph Cossman

May 20

In 1570, cartographer Abraham Ortelius publishes the first atlas

> As long as we have hope, we have direction, the energy to move, and the map to move by.
>
> —Lao Tzu

May 21

In 1927, pilot Charles Lindbergh completes the first solo nonstop flight across the Atlantic Ocean

> Time is no longer endless or the horizon destitute of hope.
>
> —Charles Lindbergh

May 22

In 1967, Mister Rogers' Neighborhood *debuts on PBS television*

> You are full of unshaped dreams. You are laden with beginnings… There is hope in you…
>
> —Lola Ridge

May 23

In 1785, Benjamin Franklin announces his invention of bifocals

You are not here merely to make a living. You are here in order to enable the world to live more amply, with greater vision, with a finer spirit of hope and achievement. You are here to enrich the world, and you impoverish yourself if you forget the errand.

—Woodrow Wilson

May 24

In 1844, Samuel F.B. Morse formally opens America's first telegraph line

Technology isn't the enemy, it is our ally, but only if we adopt a new model that puts people before profit. I realize that we seem far from that model, but I have seen it in action, and it is a beautiful thing. So I'm not willing to give up yet. Hope is the last thing to die.

—Justin Sane

May 25

In 1803, American philosopher Ralph Waldo Emerson is born

Do that which is assigned to you, and you cannot hope too much or dare too much.

—Ralph Waldo Emerson

May 26

In 1937, San Francisco's Golden Gate Bridge opens

Here's to the bridge-builders, the hand-holders, the light-bringers, those extraordinary souls wrapped in ordinary lives who quietly weave threads of humanity into an inhumane world. They are the unsung heroes in a world at war with itself. They are the whisperers of hope that peace is possible. Look for them in this present darkness. Light your candle with their flame. And then go. Build bridges. Hold hands. Bring light to a dark and desperate world. Be the hero you are looking for. Peace is possible. It begins with us.

—L.R. Knost

May 27

In 1907, American biologist and conservationist Rachel Carson is born

Where flowers bloom, so does hope.

—Lady Bird Johnson

May 28

In 1888, athlete Jim Thorpe is born, the first Native American to win an Olympic gold medal for the United States

The fire of hope almost went out; we have to rekindle it.

—Chief Red Cloud of the Oglala Dakota tribe

May 29

In 1953, New Zealand's Edmund Hillary and Sherpa Tenzing Norgay become the first men to reach the top of Mount Everest

The pursuit of science has often been compared to the scaling of mountains, high and not so high. But who amongst us can hope, even in imagination, to scale the Everest and reach its summit when the sky is blue and the air is still, and in the stillness of the air survey the entire Himalayan range in the dazzling white of the snow stretching to infinity? None of us can hope for a comparable vision of nature and of the universe around us. But there is nothing mean or lowly in standing in the valley below and awaiting the sun to rise over Kinchinjunga.

—Subrahmanijan Chandrasekhar

May 30

In 1911, the first Indianapolis 500 race takes place and is won by Ray Harroun

To travel hopefully is better than to arrive.

—Sir James Jeans

May 31

In 1898, American minister and author of The Power of
Positive Thinking *Norman Vincent Peale is born*

> Never talk defeat. Use words like hope, belief, faith, victory.
> —Norman Vincent Peale

June 1

In 1938, Superman, the world's first superhero, debuts in
Action Comics

> Once you choose hope, anything is possible.
> —Christopher Reeve

June 2

In 1966, the US space probe Surveyor 1 *lands on the moon and
sends photographs back of the moon's surface*

> When hope is fleeting, stop for a moment and visualize, in
> a sky of silver, the crescent of a lavender moon. Imagine
> it—delicate, slim, precise, like a paper-thin slice from
> a cabochon jewel. It may not be very useful, but it is
> beautiful. And sometimes it is enough.
>
> —Vera Nazarian

June 3

In 1992, the UN "Earth Summit" conference on world environmental protection opens in Rio de Janeiro

It's important for me to have hope because that's my job as a parent, to have hope for my kids, that we're not going to leave them in a world that's in shambles, that's a chaotic place, that's a dangerous place.

—James Cameron

June 4

In 1919, the US Senate passes the Women's Suffrage bill

We must vote for hope, vote for life, vote for a brighter future for all of our loved ones.

—Ed Markey

June 5

In 1851, Uncle Tom's Cabin *by Harriet Beecher Stowe is published*

I feel now that the time is come when even a woman or a child who can speak a word for freedom and humanity is bound to speak… I hope every woman who can write will not be silent.

—Harriet Beecher Stowe

June 6

In 1930, frozen foods are sold for the first time, making food more affordable and accessible

Hope can be defined as "the belief that circumstances in the future will be better." It allows us to be optimistic of a positive outcome and increases our chances of realizing our goals and dreams.

—Norbert Juma

June 7

In 1914, the first vessel passes through the Panama Canal

Hope spurs humans everywhere to work harder, to endure more now that the future may be better.

—Dwight D. Eisenhower

June 8

In 1789, James Madison introduces the Bill of Rights in the US House of Representatives

The happy Union of these States is a wonder; their Constitution a miracle; their example the hope of Liberty throughout the world.

—James Madison

June 9

In 1549, the English Book of Common Prayer *is produced, the first time a book of worship service is published in English*

> My heart, therefore, is glad, and my spirit rejoices;
> my body also shall rest in hope.
> You will show me the path of life;
> in your presence there is fullness of joy,
> and in your right hand are pleasures for evermore.
>
> —From the *Book of Common Prayer*

June 10

In 1948, Chuck Yeager becomes the first person to fly faster than the speed of sound

> My hope for you…I hope life gives you wings, and you
> have the courage to use them.
>
> —Christy Ann Martine

June 11

In 1910, French researcher and pioneer of marine conservation Jacques Cousteau is born

> The sea, the great unifier, is man's only hope. Now, as
> never before, the old phrase has a literal meaning: We are
> all in the same boat.
>
> —Jacques Yves Cousteau

June 12

In 1667, the first human blood transfusion is administered by Dr. Jean Baptiste

The funny thing about hope: When she gets into your blood, she never leaves you.

—The character of Land Lady in an episode of *NCIS*

June 13

In 1967, Thurgood Marshall is nominated to be the first African American member of the US Supreme Court

Unless our children begin to learn together, there is little hope that our people will ever begin to live together.

—Thurgood Marshall

June 14

In 1922, Warren G. Harding becomes the first US president to be heard on the radio

When one surveys the world about him after the great storm, noting the marks of destruction and yet rejoicing in the ruggedness of the things which withstood it, if he is an American, he breathes the clarified atmosphere with a strange mingling of regret and new hope.

—From Warren G. Harding's inaugural address

June 15

In 1924, Native Americans are proclaimed United States citizens

> May the stars carry your sadness away,
> May the flowers fill your heart with beauty,
> May hope forever wipe away your tears,
> And, above all, may silence make you strong.
>
> —Chief Dan George, Tsleil-Waututh Nation

June 16

In 1917, Katharine Graham, publisher of the Washington Post, *as well as the first-ever female CEO of a Fortune 500 company, is born*

> [Katharine Graham] later wrote eloquently of her tendency—and the tendency of all women—to apologize, her struggle to please those around her. But when it came time to act—as surprised as she was that she was there, in her position—she did. It's something we all hope we can do.
>
> —Vasugi V. Ganeshananthan

June 17

In 1885, the Statue of Liberty arrives in New York City aboard the French ship Isere

> Nearly all Americans have ancestors who braved the oceans—liberty-loving risk-takers in search of an ideal— [in] the largest voluntary migrations in recorded history. Across the Pacific, across the Atlantic, they came from every point on the compass—many passing beneath the Statue of Liberty—with fear and vision, with sorrow and adventure, fleeing tyranny or terror, seeking haven, and all seeking hope… Immigration is not just a link to America's past; it's also a bridge to America's future.
>
> —George H. W. Bush

June 18

In 1983, Sally Ride becomes the first American woman in space

> Hope is the little pebble in
> your empty palm that had
> vanished
> but where
> someone
> somewhere
> Tossed it in the air
> It reached the starry skies
>
> —Jan Skakel

June 19

In 1623, French physicist and philosopher Blaise Pascal is born

> Love knows no limit to its endurance, no end to its trust, no fading of its hope; it can outlast anything. Love still stands when all else has fallen.
>
> —I Corinthians 13, as adapted by Blaise Pascal

June 20

In 1214, England's University of Oxford receives its charter

> Rome has been called the "Sacred City"—might not our Oxford be called so too? There is an air about it, resonant of joy and hope: It speaks with a thousand tongues to the heart: it waves its mighty shadow over the imagination: it stands in lowly sublimity on the "hill of ages" and points with prophetic fingers to the sky... Its streets are paved with the names of learning that can never wear out: Its green quadrangles breathe the silence of thought.
>
> —William Hazlitt

SUMMER

Summer was here again....
Summers had a logic all their own
and they always brought something out in me....
Summer was a book of hope.

—Benjamin Alire Saenz

June 21

In 2001, Mexican artist Frida Kahlo is the first Hispanic woman to be honored on a US postage stamp

Árbol de la esperanza, mantente firme.
Tree of hope, stand firm.

—Frida Kahlo

June 22

In 1970, the Twenty-Sixth Amendment is passed, which lowered the voting age in the United States to eighteen

To vote is to hope.

—Mary Schmich

June 23

In 1940, American polio survivor turned Olympic medalist Wilma Rudolph is born

Hope can be a powerful force. Maybe there's no actual magic in it, but when you know what you hope for most and hold it like a light within you, you can make things happen, almost like magic.

—Laini Taylor

June 24

In 1916, Canadian American actress Mary Pickford becomes the first female film star to get a million-dollar contract

Hope is the companion of power, and mother of success; for who so hopes strongly has within him the gift of miracles.

—Samuel Smiles

June 25

In 1993, Kim Campbell takes office as the first female prime minister of Canada

Canadians want to see real hope restored, not false hopes raised.

—Kim Campbell

June 26

In 1819, a patent for the bicycle is granted to American William K. Clarkson Jr.

When the spirits are low, when the day appears dark, when work becomes monotonous, when hope hardly seems worth having, just mount a bicycle and go out for a spin down the road, without thought on anything but the ride you are taking.

—Sir Arthur Conan Doyle

June 27

In 1880, American author Helen Keller is born; she becomes deaf and blind at nineteen months old

Optimism is the faith that leads to achievement. Nothing can be done without hope and confidence.

—Helen Keller

June 28

In 1894, Labor Day becomes a national holiday in the United States

There is precious little hope to be got out of whatever keeps us industrious, but there is a chance for us whenever we cease work and become stargazers.

—H.M. Tomlinson

June 29

In 2007, Apple Computer releases the iPhone in the United States

I decided to take a calligraphy class to learn how to do this. It was beautiful, historical, artistically subtle in a way that science can't capture, and I found it fascinating. None of this had even a hope of any practical application in my life. But ten years later, when we were designing the first Macintosh computer, it all came back to me.

—Steve Jobs

June 30

In 1997, Harry Potter and the Philosopher's Stone *is published after being rejected twelve times, the first novel in author J.K. Rowling's Harry Potter series*

> Time is short, and unless the few of us who know the truth do not stand united, there is no hope for any of us.
>
> —Albus Dumbledore, a character in *Harry Potter and the Goblet of Fire* by J.K. Rowling

July 1

In 1966, the Medicare federal insurance program goes into effect in the United States

> We need never be hopeless because we can never be irreparably broken.
>
> —John Green

July 2

In 1964, US President Lyndon Johnson signs the Civil Rights Act, prohibiting segregation in public places

> This Civil Rights Act is a challenge to all of us to go to work in our communities and our states, in our homes and in our hearts, to eliminate the last vestiges of injustice in our beloved country. So tonight, I urge every public official,

every religious leader, every business and professional man, every working man, every housewife—I urge every American—to join in this effort to bring justice and hope to all our people, and to bring peace to our land.

—Lyndon Johnson

July 3

In 2005, a national law legalizing same-sex marriage in Spain goes into effect

Marriage responds to the universal fear that a lonely person might call out only to find no one there. It offers the hope of companionship and understanding and assurance that while both still live, there will be someone to care for the other.

—Justice Anthony Kennedy, on same-sex marriage

July 4

In 1776, the Declaration of Independence is approved by the US Congress

Our only hope for our collective liberation is a politics of solidarity rooted in love.

—Michelle Alexander

July 5

In 1865, William Booth starts the Salvation Army in London

Where there is no hope, it is incumbent on us to invent it.

—Albert Camus

July 6

In 1935, Tenzin Gyatso, the fourteenth Dalai Lama, is born in China

In the final analysis, the hope of every person is simply peace of mind.

—The Dalai Lama

July 7

In 1981, the nomination of Sandra Day O'Connor to become the first female Supreme Court justice is announced by US President Ronald Reagan

I hope that I have inspired young people about civic engagement and helped pave the pathway for women who may have faced obstacles pursuing their careers.

—Sandra Day O'Connor

July 8

In 1933, the Public Works Administration becomes effective in the United States

> In these days of difficulty, we Americans everywhere must and shall choose the path of social justice...the path of faith, the path of hope, and the path of love toward our fellow man.
>
> —Franklin D. Roosevelt

July 9

In 1971, US Secretary of State Henry Kissinger visits the People's Republic of China to negotiate détente between the US and China

> Hope is like a path in the countryside. Originally, there is nothing—but as people walk this way again and again, a path appears.
>
> —Lu Xun

July 10

In 1928, American entrepreneur George Eastman first demonstrates color motion pictures

> Thankfully, God has shown us that hope, in its million different forms, always springs from three primary colors: justice, mercy, and love.
>
> —Richard Dahlstrom

July 11

In 1900, England's Charlotte Cooper becomes the first female Olympic tennis champion and the first individual female Olympic champion in any sport

> Love recognizes no barriers. It jumps hurdles, leaps fences, penetrates walls to arrive at its destination full of hope.
>
> —Maya Angelou

July 12

In 1933, a minimum wage of forty cents per hour was established in the United States

> Our human compassion binds us the one to the other—not in pity or patronizingly, but as human beings who have learnt how to turn our common suffering into hope for the future.
>
> —Nelson Mandela

July 13

In 1985, two simultaneous Live AID concerts, one in London and one in Philadelphia, raise over seventy-five million dollars for famine victims in Africa

> Live AID on July 13, 1985, was "The Day the Music Changed the World." We can change the world again in

2020. We cannot hope for our political leaders to take action on these emergencies; we have to do it ourselves.

—From the press release for the LiveHope Festival, which took place online because of COVID-19

July 14

In 1912, American folksinger Woody Guthrie is born

The note of hope is the only note that can help us or save us from falling to the bottom of the heap of evolution, because, largely, about all a human being is, anyway, is just a hoping machine.

—Woodie Guthrie

July 15

In 1606, Dutch artist Rembrandt van Rijn is born

The main thing is to be moved, to love, to hope, to tremble, to live.

—Auguste Rodin

July 16

In 1194, Saint Clare of Assisi, founder of the Order of Poor Ladies, is born in Italy

Our body is not made of iron. Our strength is not that of stone. Live and hope in the Lord, and let your service be according to reason.

—Saint Clare of Assisi

July 17

In 1453, the Hundred Years' Years War ends when the French defeat the English at Castillon, France

L'espérance est un acte de foi.
Hope is an act of faith.

—Marcel Proust

July 18

In 1918, South African politician Nelson Mandela is born

May your choices reflect your hopes, not your fears.

—Nelson Mandela

July 19

In 1984, Geraldine Ferraro becomes the first woman chosen by a major political party to run for the office of US vice president

You just have to hold out hope.

—Geraldine Ferraro

July 20

In 1969, American astronaut Neil Armstrong is the first man to set foot on the moon's surface

Life affords no higher pleasures than that of surmounting difficulties, passing from one step of success to another, forming new wishes and seeing them gratified. He that labors in any great or laudable undertaking has his fatigues first supported by hope and aftermath rewarded by joy.

—Samuel Johnson

July 21

In 1957, American Althea Gibson becomes the first Black woman to win a major US tennis title

I hope that I have accomplished just one thing: that I have been a credit to tennis and my country.

—Althea Gibson

July 22

In 1890, Rose Kennedy—mother of a US president and two US senators—is born in Boston

What greater aspiration and challenge are there for a mother than the hope of raising a great son or daughter?

—Rose Kennedy

July 23

In 1904, the ice-cream cone is invented by Charles E. Menches at the Louisiana Purchase Exposition

I hope your only rocky road is chocolate.

—Amanda Mosher

July 24

In 1897, American aviator Amelia Earhart is born

For the economic structure we have built up is all too often a barrier between the world's work and the workers. If the younger generation finds the hurdle too absurdly high, I hope it will not hesitate to tear it down and substitute a social order in which the desire to work and learn carries with it the opportunity to do so.

—Amelia Earhart

July 25

In 1943, Italian dictator Benito Mussolini is overthrown

Finché c'è vita c'è speranza:
As long as there is life there is hope.

—Italian proverb

July 26

In 1875, Swiss psychiatrist and psychoanalyst Carl Gustav Jung is born

> Faith, hope, love, and insight are the highest achievements of human effort. They are found—given—by experience.
>
> —Carl Gustav Jung

July 27

In 1953, the armistice agreement ending the Korean War is signed at Panmunjon, Korea

> It is our responsibility to counter stories of fear with stories of hope, to say: It is more about what unites us than what divides us.
>
> —Darynell Rodriguez Torres

July 28

In 1959, after Hawaii's first US election, Hiram Fong and Daniel Inouye become the first Asian Americans in Congress representing Hawaii

> I hope that all leaders in this country will be innovative in trying to find ways to reach out to people to challenge their best instincts as opposed to playing to their worst instincts.
>
> —Bill Bradley

July 29

In 1958, the National Aeronautics and Space Administration (NASA) is authorized by the US Congress

It is difficult to say what is impossible, for the dream of yesterday is the hope of today and reality of tomorrow.

—Robert Goddard

July 30

In 1863, American inventor and founder of the Ford Motor Company Henry Ford is born

If money is your hope for independence, you will never have it. The only real security that a man can have in this world is a reserve of knowledge, experience, and ability.

—Henry Ford

July 31

In 1968, the African American character of Franklin makes his first appearance in the Peanuts *comic strip*

A whole stack of memories never equal one little hope.

—Charles Schulz

August 1

In 1972, the first article exposing the Watergate scandal by Washington Post *reporters Carl Bernstein and Bob Woodward is published*

There is hope: in a fiercely independent Supreme Court, a crusading free press, and an absolute commitment to representative democracy.

—Mark Tully

August 2

In 1870, the world's first subway opens in London

To live on a day-to-day basis is insufficient for human beings; we need to transcend, transport, escape; we need meaning, understanding, and explanation; we need to see overall patterns in our lives. We need hope, the sense of a future. And we need freedom (or, at least, the illusion of freedom) to get beyond ourselves, whether with telescopes and microscopes and our ever-burgeoning technology, or in states of mind that allow us to travel to other worlds, to rise above our immediate surroundings.

—Oliver Sacks

August 3

In 1936, African American athlete Jesse Owens wins the first of his four Olympic gold medals in Berlin, "single-handedly crushing Hitler's myth of Aryan supremacy"

Championships are mythical. The real champions are those who live through what they are taught in their homes and churches. The attitude that "We've got to win" in sports must be changed. Teach your youngsters, who are the future hope of America, the importance of love, respect, dedication, determination, self-sacrifice, self-discipline, and good attitude. That's the road up the ladder to the championships.

—Jesse Owens

August 4

In 1961, the first African American US president, Barack Obama, is born

Hope is that thing inside us that insists, despite all the evidence to the contrary, that something better awaits us if we have the courage to reach for it and to work for it and to fight for it.

—Barack Obama

August 5

In 1858, the first transatlantic cable service is opened when the UK's Queen Victoria exchanges greetings with US President James Buchanan

I am prepared for the worst, but hope for the best.

—Benjamin Disraeli

August 6

In 1926, US swimmer Gertrude Ederle becomes the first woman to swim the English Channel

…in the midst of near despair, something has happened beneath the surface. A bright little flashing fish of hope has flicked silver fins and the water is bright and suddenly I am returned to a state of love again….

I've learned that…I will submerge in darkness and misery, but that I won't stay submerged. And each time something has been learned under the waters…

—Madeleine L'Engle

August 7

In 1938, physician and antiwar activist Helen Caldicott is born in Australia

On one hand, I'm an optimistic pessimist. On the other, I'm a pessimistic optimist. But while there's life, there's still hope, and I wouldn't be doing what I'm doing if I didn't think there was still hope.

—Helen Caldicott

August 8

In 1786, Mont Blanc, Europe's tallest peak, is climbed for the first time by Jacques Balmat and Michel Paccard

What advantages do we hope to gain [from climbing mountains]? Naturally, there is the pleasure we get from the climbing process itself and from our victories, but as well as the delights of exercise in a mountain environment, there is also the process, coming every time as a surprise, of self-discovery deepening a little further with every climb: who we are, how far we can go, what is our potential, where are the limits of our technique, our strength, our skill, our mountaineering sense: discoveries whose acceptance means that, if necessary, we may turn back and return another time, several times if need be—Tomorrow is a new day.

—Gaston Rebuffat, from *The Mont Blanc Massif: The Hundred Finest Routes*

August 9

In 1483, the Sistine Chapel opens in Italy

Architects and painters, sculptors and musicians, filmmakers and writers, photographers and poets, artists of every discipline, are called to shine beauty especially where darkness or gray dominates everyday life… [They] are the custodians of beauty, heralds and witnesses of hope for humanity. I invite you, therefore, to cherish beauty, and beauty will heal the many wounds that mark the hearts and souls of the men and women of our day.

—Pope Francis

August 10

In 1846, the Smithsonian Institution is chartered by the US Congress

…As these doors open, it is my hope that each and every person who visits this beautiful museum will walk away deeply inspired, filled with a greater respect for the dignity and the worth of every human being and a stronger commitment to the ideals of justice, equality, and true democracy.

—John Lewis, on the opening of the Smithsonian's National Museum of African American History and Culture in 2016

August 11

In 1941, the Atlantic Charter is signed by US President Franklin D. Roosevelt and British Prime Minister Winston Churchill

Nourish your hopes, but do not overlook realities.

—Winston Churchill

August 12

In 1877, American inventor Thomas Edison creates the phonograph and makes the first sound recording

Man is a creature of hope and invention, both of which belie the idea that things cannot be changed.

—Tom Clancy

August 13

In 1913, stainless steel is invented by English metallurgist Harry Brearley

The symbol of the House of El means "Hope." Embodied within that hope is the fundamental belief in the potential of every person to be a force for good. That's what you can bring them.

—Superman's father Jor-El, *Man of Steel*

August 14

In 1945, US President Harry Truman announces that Japan has surrendered, ending World War II

You may say I'm a dreamer
but I'm not the only one
I hope someday you'll join us
And the world will live as one

—John Lennon, "Imagine"

August 15

In 1969, the Woodstock Music and Art Festival begins in Bethel, New York

Hope is hearing the music of the future. Faith is to dance to it.

—Ruben Alves

August 16

In 1913, Israeli Prime Minister Menachem Begin is born

You rise, you struggle, you make sacrifices to achieve and guarantee the prospect and hope of living in peace—for you and your people, for your children and their children.

—Menachem Begin, while accepting the Nobel Peace Prize

August 17

In 1903, American Joseph Pulitzer donates one million dollars to Columbia University, which went on to found the Pulitzer Prizes in 1916 in his name

> Every one of you is a shining example of Pulitzer's ideals: a trained intelligence, courage, craft, and dedication.... Throughout the country, despite the trends in reading, there is actually a powerful hunger for your work—for hard-hitting journalism, moving fiction, unsettling drama, and spirit-lifting song. It's time to think big again. It's time for all the writers here assembled and for this family of news organizations to reach even harder for the audiences who have fallen away. As they do so, may the journalists of the future, like our predecessors, forge bonds among themselves, the people, and the poets. Along this path lies hope.
>
> —Danielle Allen, excerpted from her Pulitzer Centennial Keynote speech, 2016

August 18

In 1587, Virginia Dare is born, the first English child born in America

> A new baby is like the beginning of all things—wonder, hope, a dream of possibilities.
>
> —Eda J. LeShan

August 19

In 1946, US President Bill Clinton is born

> …I learned that everyone has a story—of dreams and nightmares, hope and heartache, love and loss, courage and fear, sacrifice and selfishness. All my life I've been interested in other people's stories. I wanted to know them, understand them, feel them. When I grew up into politics, I always felt the main point of my work was to give people a chance to have better stories.
>
> —Bill Clinton

August 20

In 1913, Adolphe Pegoud of France is the first pilot to parachute from an aircraft

> Hope. It helps *you* to float—to rise above your circumstances. It helps you to be lifted above your worries, your doubts, your fears.
>
> —Rosheeda Lee

August 21

In 1888, American inventor William Seward Burroughs patents the adding machine

> Math may not teach us how to add love or subtract hate; but it gives us hope that every problem has a solution.
>
> —Anonymous

August 22

*In 1864, the Red Cross is formed with the signing of the first
Geneva Convention treaty*

My mother used to say, a long time ago, whenever there
would be any catastrophe that was on the air, she would
say, "Always look for the helpers. Because if you look for
the helpers, you'll know that there's hope."

—*Fred Rogers*

August 23

In 1948, the World Council of Churches is founded

We judge of man's wisdom by his hope.

—Ralph Waldo Emerson

August 24

*In 1949, the North Atlantic Treaty Organization (NATO)
is founded*

…America truly is the world's indispensable nation. There
are times when only America can make the difference
between war and peace, between freedom and repression,
between hope and fear. We cannot and should not try to be
the world's policeman. But where our interests and values
are clearly at stake, and where we can make a difference, we
must act and lead.

—Bill Clinton in a 1996 address on NATO

August 25

In 1916, the National Park Service is established as part of the US Department of the Interior

> Plant seeds of happiness, hope, success, and love; it will all come back to you in abundance. This is the law of nature.
>
> —Steve Maraboli

August 26

In 1843, American inventor Charles Thurber patents a typewriter

> I seat myself at the typewriter and hope, and lurk.
>
> —Mignon G. Eberhart

August 27

In 1910, Albanian missionary Mother Teresa, who helped the desperate in India for decades, is born

> We want to create hope for the person…we must give hope, always hope.
>
> —Mother Teresa

August 28

In 1963, Martin Luther King Jr. delivers his "I Have a Dream" speech

...This is our hope. This is the faith with which I return. With this faith, we will be able to hew out of the mountain of despair a stone of hope.

—Dr. Martin Luther King Jr.

August 29

In 1833, Britain's first Factory Act becomes law to "regulate the Labour of Children and young Persons in the Mills and Factories of the United Kingdom"

When you put faith, hope, and love together, you can raise positive kids in a negative world.

—Zig Ziglar

August 30

In 1983, Guion Bluford becomes the first African American astronaut in space

On behalf of all our people, I want to thank you all for your courage, your commitment to space research. You've set a fine example for all our young people who represent our hope for the future.

—President Ronald Reagan, during a call to the space-shuttle crew that included Guion Bluford

August 31

*In 1870, Italian physician and educator Maria
Montessori is born*

> The child is capable of developing and giving us tangible
> proof of the possibility of a better humanity. He has shown
> us the true process of construction of the human being.
> We have seen children totally change as they acquire a love
> for things and as their sense of order, discipline, and self-
> control develops within them…. The child is both a hope
> and a promise for mankind.
>
> —Maria Montessori

September 1

*In 1897, the Boston Subway opens, becoming the first
underground rapid-transit system in North America*

> Hope can be bruised and battered. It can be forced
> underground and even rendered unconscious, but hope
> cannot be killed.
>
> —Neal Shusterman

September 2

In 1992, the United States and Russia agree to a joint venture to build a space station

Instead of talking in the hope that people will listen, try listening in the hope that people will talk.

—Mardy Grothe

September 3

In 1783, the Revolutionary War between the United States and Great Britain officially ends with the Treaty of Paris

I hope…that all mankind will at length…have reason and sense enough to settle their differences without cutting throats.

—Benjamin Franklin

September 4

In 1998, Google is founded by Larry Page and Sergey Brin, both students at Stanford University

The difference between hope and despair is a different way of telling stories from the same facts.

—Alain de Botton

September 5

*In 1774, the first Continental Congress in America opens
in Philadelphia*

> You will never know how much it cost the present
> Generation to preserve your Freedom! I hope you will
> make good use of it.
>
> —John Adams

September 6

*In 1757, Gilbert de Motier, the Marquis de Lafayette, French
soldier and statesman, is born*

> I hope our people will keep up their courage. I have no
> doubt of their finally succeeding by the blessing of *God*,
> nor have I any doubt that so good a cause will fail of
> that blessing.
>
> —Benjamin Franklin

September 7

*In 1860, American folk artist Grandma Moses (née Anna Mary
Robertson) is born*

> What a strange thing is memory, and hope; one looks
> backward, the other forward; one is of today, the other
> of tomorrow.
>
> —Grandma Moses

September 8

In 1986, The Oprah Winfrey Show *first airs*

> Forgiveness is giving up the hope that the past could have been any different; it's accepting the past for what it was and using this moment and this time to help yourself move forward.

—Oprah Winfrey

September 9

In 1839, the first glass-plate photograph is taken by English inventor John Herschel

> Hope is a straw hat hanging beside a window covered with frost.

—Margaret George

September 10

In 1918, the German Shepherd turned film star Rin Tin Tin is born in France

> You can always find hope in a dog's eyes.

—Anonymous

September 11

In 1893, the first conference of the World Parliament of Religions is held in Chicago

> Imagine what we could build together if we used faith, hope, and love as our building materials?
>
> —Anonymous

September 12

In 1940, ancient cave paintings are discovered in Lascaux, France

> Art is the highest form of hope.
>
> —Gerhard Richter

September 13

In 1948, Margaret Chase Smith becomes the first woman elected to both houses of the US Congress when she is elected to the Senate

> I speak as briefly as possible because too much harm has already been done with irresponsible words of bitterness and selfish political opportunism. I speak as simply as possible because the issue is too great to be obscured by eloquence. I speak simply and briefly in the hope that my words will be taken to heart.
>
> — Margaret Chase Smith, from her "Declaration of Conscience" rebuttal against Senator Joseph McCarthy

September 14

In 1879, American birth-control activist, writer, and nurse Margaret Sanger is born

> The real hope of the world lies in putting as painstaking thought into the business of mating as we do into other big businesses.

—Margaret Sanger

September 15

In 1928, Scottish physician and microbiologist Alexander Fleming discovers penicillin

> There is no medicine like hope, no incentive so great, and no tonic so powerful as expectation of something better tomorrow.

—Orison Swett Marden

September 16

In 1976, the American Episcopal Church approves ordination of women as priests and bishops

> It is my hope that inter-religious and ecumenical cooperation will demonstrate that men and women do not have to forsake their identity, whether ethnic or religious, in order to live in harmony with their brothers and sisters. If we are honest in presenting our convictions, we will be able to see more clearly what we hold in common.

—Pope Francis

September 17

In 1980, the Solidarity labor union forms in Poland

Solidarity does not assume that our struggles are the same struggles, or that our pain is the same pain, or that our hope is for the same future. Solidarity involves commitment and work, as well as the recognition that even if we do not have the same feelings, or the same lives, or the same bodies, we do live on common ground.

—Sara Ahmed

September 18

In 1997, American philanthropist Ted Turner gives one billion dollars to the United Nations, creating the charitable United Nations Foundation

In faith and hope the world will disagree, but all mankind's concern is charity.

—Alexander Pope

September 19

In 1893, New Zealand becomes the first country to grant all women the right to vote

I hope that [my daughter] doesn't feel any limitations; that she doesn't have any sense of what girls can or can't do; that it's just not even a concept for her.

—Jacinda Ardern, prime minister of New Zealand

September 20

In 1973, American tennis player Billie Jean King defeats Bobby Riggs in the "Battle of the Sexes" tennis match

Sports have the power to change the world. It has the power to inspire, the power to unite people in a way that little else does. It speaks to youth in a language they understand. Sports can create hope, where there was once only despair….

—Nelson Mandela

September 21

In 1897, the New York Sun *runs the "Yes, Virginia, There Is a Santa Claus" editorial by Francis Church*

Church was a veteran newspaperman. (He died nine years later at the age of sixty-seven.) He had been a Civil War correspondent. The country in 1897 had just emerged from a devastating six-year economic depression that rivaled the Great Depression a mere thirty years later. He had seen his share of dark times.

Church could have tossed off some tired collection of comforting and unconvincing clichés—but he didn't. Why he didn't is the marvel and the mystery. Instead of condescending claptrap, he embraced the challenge.

Whatever the reason, he chose instead to write a testament to hope.

—Ken Trainor

September 22

In 1961, US President John F. Kennedy signs a congressional act establishing the Peace Corps

The Peace Corps represents some, if not all, of the best virtues in this society. It stands for everything that America has ever stood for. It stands for everything we believe in and hope to achieve in the world.

—Sargent Shriver

AUTUMN

How could you not be hopeful
if you've got a tree around?

—Ross Spears

September 23

In 1949, American singer-songwriter Bruce Springsteen is born

All people have is hope. That's what brings the next day and whatever that day may bring…a hope grounded in the real world of living, friendship, work, family…

—Bruce Springsteen

September 24

In 1936, American puppeteer and Muppets creator Jim Henson is born

When I was young, my ambition was to be one of the people who made a difference in this world. My hope is to leave the world a little better for having been there.

—Jim Henson

September 25

In 1931, American broadcaster Barbara Walters, the first female television anchor of an evening news show, is born

I don't believe that the best is yet to come, and I don't know why at this point in my life, at my oldest, I am more content than I have ever been. If that gives anybody hope—I don't feel depressed, even though I know that my working life is going to be less and that probably

my greatest work is behind me. I am very happy. I have
accomplished what I wanted to accomplish; my [daughter]
is fine and happy and successful in her life. ... I have great
freedom in my life now.

—Barbara Walters

September 26

In 1981, legendary American tennis player Serena
Williams is born

Growing up, I wasn't the richest, but I had a rich family
in spirit. Standing here with nineteen championships is
something I never thought would happen. I went on a court
just with a ball and a racket and with a hope.

—Serena Williams

September 27

In 1962, American marine biologist and ecologist Rachel Carson
publishes Silent Spring, *her seminal work on the environmental*
dangers of pesticide use

During the wild uncertainty of a frightened land, Spring
reached out her mystical hand; willing to give us hope.

—Angie Weiland-Crosby

September 28

In 551 BC, Chinese philosopher Confucius is born

Education breeds confidence. Confidence breeds hope.
Hope breeds peace.

—Confucius

September 29

*In 1943, Polish statesman and Nobel Peace Prize winner Lech
Walesa is born*

The hope of the nation, which throughout the nineteenth
century had not for a moment reconciled itself with the loss
of independence, and fighting for its own freedom, fought
at the same time for the freedom of other nations.

—Lech Walesa

September 30

*In 1846, anesthetic ether is used for the first time (to extract a
tooth) by American dentist Dr. William Morton*

Hope is our life anesthesia.

—Kazimierz Matan

October 1

In 1924, Jimmy Carter, the thirty-ninth US president, is born

Ours was the first nation to be founded on the idea that all are created equal and all deserve equal treatment under the law. Despite our missteps and shortcomings, these ideals still inspire hope among the oppressed and give us pride in being Americans.

—Jimmy Carter

October 2

In 1869, Indian political ethicist, leader, and attorney Mahatma Gandhi is born

I claim to be an average man of less than average ability.... I have not the shadow of a doubt that any man or woman can achieve what I have, if he or she would make the same effort and cultivate the same hope and faith.

—Mahatma Gandhi

October 3

In 1951, Kathy Sullivan, the first American woman to walk in space, is born

Being an astronaut is a wonderful career. I feel very privileged. But what I really hope for young people is that they find a career they are passionate about, something that's challenging and worthwhile.

—Ellen Ochoa, former astronaut and former director of the Johnson Space Center

October 4

In 1181 or 1182, Saint Francis of Assisi is born in Italy

Lord, make me an instrument of Thy peace. Where there is hatred, let me sow love; where there is injury, pardon; where there is doubt, faith; where there is despair, hope; where there is sadness, joy; where there is darkness, light.

O Divine Master, grant that I may not so much seek to be consoled, as to console; not so much to be understood, as to understand; not so much to be loved, as to love. For it is in giving that we receive, it is in pardoning that we are pardoned, it is in dying that we are born again to eternal life.

—St. Francis of Assisi

October 5

In 1936, playwright-dissident and Czech Republic President Vaclav Havel is born

The communist type of totalitarian system has left…a legacy of countless dead, an infinite spectrum of human suffering, profound economic decline and, above all, enormous human humiliation…. It has [also] given us something positive—a special capacity to look from time to time somewhat further than someone who has not undergone this bitter experience. A person who cannot move and lead a somewhat normal life because he is pinned under a boulder has more time to think about his hopes than someone who is not trapped that way....

We too can offer something to you: our experience and the knowledge that has come from it.... Consciousness precedes being, and not the other way around, as the Marxists claim. For this reason, the salvation of this human world lies nowhere else than in the human heart, in the human power to reflect, in human meekness and human responsibility.

—Vaclav Havel

October 6

In 1847, Jane Eyre *by English novelist Charlotte Bronte is first published*

I remembered that the real world was wide, and that a varied field of hopes and fears, of sensations and excitements, awaited those who had the courage to go forth into its expanse, to seek real knowledge of life amidst its perils.

—Charlotte Bronte, *Jane Eyre*

October 7

In 1931, South African cleric and human rights activist Desmond Tutu is born

> Hope is being able to see that there is light despite all of the darkness.
>
> —Desmond Tutu

October 8

In 1941, American activist, minister, and politician Jesse Jackson is born

> You must never stop dreaming. Face reality, yes, but don't stop with the way things are. Dream of things as they ought to be. Dream. Face pain, but love, hope, faith, and dreams will help you rise above the pain. Use hope and imagination as weapons of survival and progress, but you keep on dreaming, young America.... Keep hope alive. Keep hope alive! Keep hope alive!
>
> —Rev. Jesse Jackson

October 9

In 1877, the American Humane Association is founded in Cleveland

> The dog is a gentleman; I hope to go to his heaven, not man's.
>
> —Mark Twain

October 10

In 1959, Pan American World Airways (Pan Am) begins regular flights around the world

Travel isn't always pretty. It isn't always comfortable. Sometimes it hurts, it even breaks your heart. But that's okay. The journey changes you; it should change you. It leaves marks on your memory, on your consciousness, on your heart, and on your body. You take something with you. Hopefully, you leave something good behind.

—Anthony Bourdain

October 11

In 1884, First Lady of the United States, diplomat, and activist Eleanor Roosevelt is born

Surely, in the light of history, it is more intelligent to hope rather than to fear, to try rather than not to try. For one thing we know beyond all doubt: Nothing has ever been achieved by the person who says, "It can't be done."

—Eleanor Roosevelt

October 12

In 1692, the Salem Witch Trials come to an end

Maybe all one can do is hope to end up with the right regrets.

—Arthur Miller

October 13

In 1773, the Whirlpool Galaxy is discovered by French astronomer Charles Messier

> We hope someday, having solved the problems we face, to join a community of galactic civilizations. This record represents our hope and our determination, and our good will in a vast and awesome universe.
>
> —Jimmy Carter

October 14

In 1964, Dr. Martin Luther King Jr. is awarded the Nobel Peace Prize for his nonviolent resistance to racial prejudice in America

> We must accept finite disappointment, but never lose infinite hope.
>
> —Dr. Martin Luther King Jr.

October 15

In 1878, the Edison Electric Light company begins its operation in America

> I'd put my money on the sun and solar energy. What a source of power! I hope we don't have to wait until oil and coal run out before we tackle that. I wish I had more years left.
>
> —Thomas Edison

October 16

In 1923, American animator Walt Disney contracts to distribute the Alice Comedies, an event which is recognized as the start of the Disney Company

> I prefer to amuse people in the hope that they will learn, [rather] than to teach them in the hope that they will have fun.
>
> —Walt Disney

October 17

In 1888, the first issue of National Geographic *magazine is released at newsstands*

> By showing up with hope to help others, I'm guaranteed that hope is present. Then my own hope increases. By creating hope for others, I end up awash in the stuff.
>
> —Anne Lamott, in the October 2018 of
> *National Geographic*

October 18

In 1842, American inventor Samuel Morse laid his first telegraph cable

> The only gleam of hope, and I can not underrate it, is from confidence in God. When I look upward it calms my apprehensions for the future, and I seem to hear a voice

saying: "If I clothe the lilies of the field, shall I not also clothe you?"

Here is my strong confidence, and I will wait patiently for the direction of Providence.

—Samuel F.B. Morse, in a letter to his wife

October 19

In 1781, British General Lord Cornwallis surrenders to General George Washington at Yorktown, Virginia, in the last battle of the American Revolution

The red and white and starry blue
Is freedom's shield and hope.

—John Philip Sousa

October 20

In 1955, English writer J.R.R. Tolkien's The Return of the King, *the last installment in* The Lord of the Rings *trilogy, is published*

Oft hope is born when all is forlorn.

—J.R.R. Tolkien, *The Return of the King*

October 21

In 1879, American inventor Thomas Edison creates the light bulb

Let the light of hope always enlighten your soul.

—Debasish Mridha

October 22

In 1966, the Supremes become the first all-female singing group to have a number-one selling album in America with The Supremes A' Go-Go

This week, my son thinks he's the Supremes—all of them. So we can scratch "straight" off the list. At least I hope we can. As a gay kid, he'll be a natural leader.

—Steve Kluger

October 23

In 1910, American Blanche S. Scott becomes the first woman to make a public solo airplane flight

She joined the small group of barnstormers on the daredevil circuit, expressing the hope that her stunts, which included three-thousand-foot "death dives," would stimulate more opportunities for women. For her aerobatics, she received as much as five thousand dollars a week. She crashed twice and explained one of them as "my fault, I was in love."

—From the 1970 *New York Times* obituary of Blanche Stuart Scott

October 24

In 1945, the United Nations is formally established less than a month after the end of World War II

If the United Nations once admits that international disputes can be settled by using force, then we will have destroyed the foundation of the organization and our best hope of establishing a world order.

—Dwight D. Eisenhower

October 25

In 1881, Spanish artist Pablo Picasso is born

The different styles I have been using in my art must not be seen as an evolution, or as steps towards an unknown ideal of painting. Everything I have ever made was made for the present and with the hope that it would always remain in the present.

—Pablo Picasso

October 26

In 1947, First Lady, US Senator, US Secretary of State, and first female presidential candidate of a major American political party Hillary Clinton is born

It is often when night looks darkest, it is often before the fever breaks that one senses the gathering momentum for change, when one feels that resurrection of hope in the midst of despair and apathy.

—Hillary Clinton

October 27

In 1904, the New York subway system officially opens

Everyone has their own New York in the heart, [a] place where there is hope for everybody.

—T.A.

October 28

In 1886, the Statue of Liberty is dedicated

Hold on in the darkness though no gleam of light
    breaks through.
Keep on dreaming dreams although they never quite
    come true.
Keep on moving forward though you don't know
    what's ahead.
Keep on keeping on though it's a lonely road ahead.

Keep on looking up towards the goal you have in view.
Keep on at the task God has given you to do.
Keep on in the hope that there are better times in store.
Keep on praying for the thing that you are waiting for.

Blessings come to those who in the turmoil of events
Seek to see the goodness of the Will of Providence.
Hold to this and never doubt. Keep head and spirits high.
You'll discover that the storm was only passing by.

Seek Love in the pity of another's woe,
In the gentle relief of another's care.
In the darkness of night and the winter's snow.
In the naked and outcast—seek love there.

—Anonymous

October 29

In 1998, seventy-seven-year-old American astronaut John Glenn becomes the oldest person to go to space

There's a lot of hope. You should run your life not by the calendar, but how you feel and what your interests are and [your] ambitions. Old folks have dreams and ambitions too, like everybody else. Don't sit on a couch someplace.

—John Glenn, responding after the shuttle had touched down to an eighty-three-year-old reporter asking if there was hope for people of his generation

October 30

In 1925, Scottish inventor John Baird makes the first televised transmission of a moving object—a fifteen-year-old office boy

Television has spread the habit of instant reaction and stimulated the hope of instant results.

—Arthur M. Schlesinger Jr.

October 31

In 1517, German priest Martin Luther posts the Ninety-Five Theses on the door of the Wittenberg Palace Church

Everything that is done in the world is done by hope.

—Martin Luther

November 1

In 1870, the US Weather Bureau (later the National Weather Service) makes its first weather forecast

God puts rainbows in the clouds so that each of us—in the dreariest and most dreaded moments—can see a possibility of hope.

—Maya Angelou

November 2

In 1920, KDKA in Pittsburgh begins regular broadcasting, making it the first commercial radio station in America

"Hello, I hope somebody is listening… If nobody is listening, am I making any sound at all?"

—Alice Oseman, *Radio Silence*

November 3

In 1507, Italy's Leonardo DaVinci is commissioned to paint the Mona Lisa

One's thoughts turn towards Hope.

—Leonardo DaVinci

November 4

In 2008, the United States elects its first African American president, Barack Obama

Hope is not blind optimism. It's not ignoring the enormity of the task ahead or the roadblocks that stand in our path. It's not sitting on the sidelines or shirking from a fight. Hope is that thing inside us that insists, despite all evidence to the contrary, that something better awaits us if we have the courage to reach for it, and to work for it, and to fight for it. Hope is the belief that destiny will not be written for us, but by us, by the men and women who are not content to settle for the world as it is, who have the courage to remake the world as it should be.

—Barack Obama

November 5

In 1974, Ella T. Grasso is elected governor of Connecticut, the first woman in the United States to be elected governor of any state without succeeding her husband

We dream to give ourselves hope. To stop dreaming—well, that's like saying you can never change your fate.

—Amy Tan, *The Hundred Secret Senses*

November 6

In 1860, Abraham Lincoln is elected the sixteenth US president

The power of hope upon human exertion, and happiness, is wonderful.

—Abraham Lincoln

November 7

In 1918, world-famous American evangelist Billy Graham is born

Perhaps the greatest psychological, spiritual, and medical need that all people have is the need for hope.

—Billy Graham

November 8

In 1895, German mechanical engineer Wilhelm Roentgen takes the first X-ray pictures

Every area of trouble gives out a ray of hope; and the one unchangeable certainty is that nothing is certain or unchangeable.

—John F. Kennedy

November 9

In 1989, the Berlin Wall comes down

Hope is always about possible future. For too long we…
have been looking backward when we hear the term *history*.
But history is about what is emerging and *can* emerge as
well as what has already emerged.

—Matthew Fox, theologian, Episcopalian priest,
and activist

November 10

In 1969, Sesame Street *makes its television debut*

Where there is life, there is hope.

—Grover, *Sesame Street*

November 11

In 1821, Russian novelist Fyodor Dostoyevsky is born

To live without hope is to cease to live.

—Fyodor Dostoyevsky

November 12

*In 1815, American women's rights leader Elizabeth Cady
Stanton is born*

Hope isn't something that we ask of others. It's something that we have to demand from ourselves.

—Amanda Gorman

November 13

In 1956, the US Supreme Court strikes down laws mandating racial segregation on public buses

I do the very best I can to look upon life with optimism and hope and looking forward to a better day.

—Rosa Parks

November 14

In 1954, Condoleezza Rice is born, the first female African American Secretary of State and the first woman to serve as a US national security advisor

Our work has only begun. In our time, we have an historic opportunity to shape a global balance of power that favors freedom and that will therefore deepen and extend the peace. And I use the word power broadly, because even more important than military and indeed economic power is the power of ideas, the power of compassion, and the power of hope.

—Condoleezza Rice

November 15

In 1837, English teacher Isaac Pitman's system of shorthand was published

Love, hope, fear, faith—these make humanity;
These are its sign and note and character.

—Robert Browning

November 16

In 1841, life preservers made of cork are patented by American inventor Napoleon Guerin

It's difficult to hold on to the life preserver of hope when storms rage in your life, but let me encourage you to tighten your grip.

—Colleen Swindoll

November 17

In 1800, the US Congress meets for the first time in the half-completed Capitol building in Washington, DC

Hope is not something that you have. Hope is something that you create, with your actions. Hope is contagious. Other people start acting in a way that has more hope.

—US Representative Alexandria Ocasio-Cortez

November 18

In 1789, Louis Daguerre, father of photography, is
born in France

> Black and white are the colors of photography. To me they
> symbolize the alternatives of hope and despair to which
> mankind is forever subjected.
>
> —Robert Frank

November 19

In 1863, Abraham Lincoln delivers the Gettysburg Address

> In giving freedom to the slave, we assure freedom to
> the free—honorable alike in what we give and what we
> preserve. We shall nobly save, or meanly lose, the last best
> hope of earth.
>
> —Abraham Lincoln

November 20

In 1942, Joe Biden, the forty-sixth US president, is born

> And together, we shall write an American story of
>   hope, not fear
> Of unity, not division
> Of light, not darkness
> An American story of decency and dignity
> Of love and of healing
> Of greatness and of goodness.

May this be the story that guides us
The story that inspires us
The story that tells ages yet to come that we answered the
    call of history
We met the moment
That democracy and hope, truth and justice, did not die on
    our watch but thrived.

—From the inaugural address of President Joe Biden

November 21

*In 1783, the first successful flight is made in a hot-air
balloon in Paris*

Hope is a helium balloon. It is a wish lantern set out into
the dark sky of night.

—Sharon Weil

November 22

*In 1819, English novelist George Eliot (born Mary Ann
Evans) is born*

There is no despair so absolute as that which comes with
the first moments of our first great sorrow, when we have
not yet known what it is to have suffered and be healed, to
have despaired and have recovered hope.

—George Eliot

November 23

In 1889, the first jukebox makes its debut in San Francisco

During the ups and downs of life, there will always be those masterpieces that fully describe what you're feeling at the present moment. There is music that lifts you up when you're sad and music that keeps you going despite all the difficulties. Motivational music can help you reach the next level and instills a feeling of courage and hope during times of despair. In short, music truly is something magical. It's therapy for the soul.

—Steve Mueller

November 24

In 1888, American self-improvement author and lecturer Dale Carnegie is born

Most of the important things in the world have been accomplished by people who have kept on trying when there seemed to be no hope at all.

—Dale Carnegie

November 25

In 1881, Pope John XXIII is born in Italy

Consult not your fears, but your hopes and your dreams.
Think not about your frustrations, but about your
unfulfilled potential.

—Pope John XXIII

November 26

*In 1607, minister and founder of Harvard College John Harvard
is born in England*

The main hope of a nation lies in the proper education of
its youth.

—Erasmus

November 27

*In 1940, Chinese American martial artist, actor/director, and
philosopher Bruce Lee is born*

It is not a shame to be knocked down by other people. The
important thing is to ask when you're being knocked down,
"Why am I being knocked down?" If a person can reflect in
this way, then there is hope for this person.

—Bruce Lee

November 28

In 1919, US-born Lady Nancy Astor is elected as the first female member of the British House of Commons

It is hopeless trying to go forward when you are looking backward.

—Nancy Astor

November 29

In 1832, American novelist and author of Little Women *Louisa May Alcott is born*

There is no other help or hope for human weakness but God's love and patience.

—Louisa May Alcott

November 30

In 1874, British politician Winston Churchill is born

All the great things are simple, and many can be expressed in a single word: freedom; justice; honor; duty; mercy; hope.

—Winston Churchill

December 1

*In 1982, the first permanent artificial heart is implanted in
Barney Clark*

While the heart beats, hope lingers.

—Alison Croggon

December 2

*In 1988, Benazir Bhutto is sworn in as the first female president
of Pakistan*

It's true that General Musharraf opposes my return,
seeing me as a symbol of democracy in the country. He is
comfortable with dictatorship. I hope better sense prevails.

—Benazir Bhutto

December 3

In 1857, Polish-British author Joseph Conrad is born

Woe to the man whose heart has not learned while young
to hope, to love—and to put its trust in life.

—Joseph Conrad

December 4

In 1791, the Observer—*the world's first Sunday newspaper—is first published*

> Half of the American people have never read a newspaper.
> Half never voted for president. One hopes it is the
> same half.
>
> —Gore Vidal

December 5

In 1901, American animator and entrepreneur Walt Disney is born

> That's what we storytellers do. We restore order with
> imagination. We instill hope again and again and again.
>
> —Walt Disney

December 6

In 1768, the Encyclopedia Britannica *is first published*

> Live, then, and be happy, beloved children of my heart, and
> never forget that until the day God will deign to reveal the
> future to man, all human wisdom is contained in these two
> words, Wait and Hope.
>
> —Alexandre Dumas

December 7

In 1873, American novelist Willa Cather is born

The mind, too, has a kind of blood; in common speech we call it hope.

—Willa Cather, in *Shadows on the Rock*

December 8

In 1765, Eli Whitney—American inventor of the cotton gin—is born

The smell when I walk into that cotton gin is hope—hope that we all make it through the season safely, hope that we'll make some money so we can do it again next year, and hope that one day one of these grandchildren will know this experience that I cherish.

—David Blakemore

December 9

In 1990, Lech Walesa, leader of the once-outlawed Solidarity movement, becomes the first democratically elected president of Poland

I hope to work harder than ever to help people around the world.

—Lech Walesa

December 10

In 1964, Martin Luther King Jr. is the youngest person ever to receive the Nobel Peace Prize

> If you lose hope, somehow you lose the vitality that keeps life moving, you lose that courage to be, that quality that helps you go on in spite of it all. And so today I still have a dream.
>
> —Dr. Martin Luther King Jr.

December 11

In 1946, the United Nations International Children's Emergency Fund (UNICEF) is founded

> Our children are our only hope for the future, but we are their only hope for their present and their future.
>
> —Zig Ziglar

December 12

In 1900, the African American national anthem, "Lift Every Voice and Sing," is composed

> Sing a song full of the faith that the dark past has taught us
> Sing a song full of the hope that the present has brought us
> Facing the rising sun of our new day begun
> Let us march on till victory is won
>
> —From "Lift Every Voice and Sing," composed by
> J. Rosamond Johnson and James Weldon Johnson

December 13

In 1920, the League of Nations establishes the International Court of Justice in The Hague

> If justice takes place, there may be hope, even in the face of a seemingly capricious divinity.
>
> —Alberto Manguel

December 14

In 1959, the Motown label is founded by Berry Gordy in Detroit, Michigan

> Many years ago, but not so long ago, there were those who said, "Well, you have three strikes against you: You're Black, you're blind, and you're poor." But God said to me, "I will make you rich in the spirit of inspiration, to inspire others as well as create music to encourage the world to a place of oneness and hope, and positivity." I believed Him and not them.
>
> —Stevie Wonder

December 15

In 1791, the first ten amendments to the Constitution, known as the Bill of Rights, are ratified

> America is hope. It is compassion. It is excellence. It is valor.
>
> —Paul Tsongas

December 16

In 1901, American anthropologist and author Margaret Mead is born

> It has been a woman's task throughout history to go on believing in life when there was almost no hope.
>
> —Margaret Mead

December 17

In 1986, Davina Thompson becomes the world's first recipient of a transplanted heart, lungs, and liver

> Without the organ donor, there is no story, no hope, no transplant. But when there is an organ donor, life springs from death, sorrow turns to hope, and a terrible loss becomes a gift.
>
> —United Network for Organ Sharing

December 18

In 1947, acclaimed American director Steven Spielberg is born

> I've always been very hopeful, which I guess isn't strange coming from me. I don't want to call myself an optimist. I want to say that I've always been full of hope. I've never lost that. I have a lot of hope for this country and for the entire world.
>
> —Steven Spielberg

December 19

In 1606, three ships leave England bound for the New World, carrying settlers who would start Jamestown, the first of the American colonies

Who dares nothing, need hope for nothing.

—Friedrich Schiller

December 20

In 1971, the first preview issue of Ms. Magazine *is published in the US, launched by American journalist Gloria Steinem*

After all, hope is a form of planning. If our hopes weren't already real within us, we couldn't even hope them.

—Gloria Steinem

December 21

In 1937, Walt Disney premieres the first full-length animated motion picture, Snow White and the Seven Dwarves

And what exactly do you think fairy tales are? They are a reminder that our lives will get better if we just hold on to hope. Your happy ending may not be what you expect; but that is what will make it so special.

—Mary Margaret Blanchard, a character in the TV series
Once Upon a Time

December 22

In 1989, Berlin's Brandenburg Gate reopens after almost thirty years of being closed

> I do not come here to lament, for I find in Berlin a message of hope, even in the shadow of this wall, a message of triumph…. As I looked out a moment ago from the Reichstag, that embodiment of German unity, I noticed words crudely spray-painted upon the wall, perhaps by a young Berliner (quote): "This wall will fall. Beliefs become reality."

> Yes, across Europe, this wall will fall, for it cannot withstand faith; it cannot withstand truth. The wall cannot withstand freedom.

> —President Ronald Reagan

December 23

In 1986, Dick Rutan and Jeana Yeager make the first nonstop flight around the world without refueling on the US plane Voyager

> A dream is the bearer of a new possibility, the enlarged horizon, the great hope.

> —Howard Thurman

December 24

*In 1814, the Treaty of Ghent is signed, ending the War of 1812
between the United States, the United Kingdom, and their allies*

So let us persevere. Peace need not be impracticable, and
war need not be inevitable. By defining our goal more
clearly, by making it seem more manageable and less
remote, we can help all peoples to see it, to draw hope from
it, and to move irresistibly toward it.

—John F. Kennedy

December 25

*In 1914, the legendary "Christmas Truce" takes place on a World
War I battlefield between British and German troops. Instead of
fighting, soldiers exchange gifts and play football*

To be hopeful in bad times is not just foolishly romantic.
It is based on the fact that human history is a history not
only of cruelty, but also of compassion, sacrifice, courage,
kindness. What we choose to emphasize in this complex
history will determine our lives. If we see only the worst, it
destroys our capacity to do something.

—Howard Zinn

December 26

In 1825, the Erie Canal opens

What an anchor is to a ship, hope is to the soul. Both ships and souls are kept safe by a firm, secure anchor that keeps holding despite turbulent winds and churning tides.

—June Hunt

December 27

In 1978, Spain becomes a democracy after forty years of dictatorship when King Juan Carlos ratifies Spain's first democratic constitution

The very least you can do in your life is figure out what you hope for. And the most you can do is live inside that hope. Not admire it from a distance but live right in it, under its roof.

—Barbara Kingsolver

December 28

In 1973, the Endangered Species Act is passed in the United States

There is still so much in the world worth fighting for. So much that is beautiful, so many wonderful people working to reverse the harm, to help alleviate the suffering. And so many young people dedicated to making this a better world. All conspiring to inspire us and to give us hope that it is not too late to turn things around, if we all do our part.

—Dr. Jane Goodall

December 29

In 1952, the first transistorized hearing aid is offered for sale in Elmsford, NY

In the night of death, hope sees a star, and listening love can hear the rustle of a wing.

—Robert Green Ingersoll

December 30

In 1972, US president Richard Nixon halts bombing of North Vietnam and announces peace talks

To love means loving the unlovable. To forgive means pardoning the unpardonable. Faith means believing the unbelievable. Hope means hoping when everything seems hopeless.

—G.K. Chesterton

December 31

In 2020, WHO grants the Pfizer/BioNTech COVID-19 vaccine emergency authorization, paving the way for worldwide distribution

Hope smiles from the threshold of the year to come, whispering, "it will be happier"…

—Alfred Lord Tennyson

Conclusion

As this book goes to press in the spring of 2021, things are beginning to feel more hopeful after a year spent shut down due to the global pandemic—vaccines are being distributed worldwide, schools are starting to reopen, and things are beginning to feel more "normal."

Yet we have an opportunity to alchemize the experience that we all have been through—to turn the dark and frightening days of the past into gold by "harvesting" them for insights and understandings that we may wish to take with us as we venture into the future.

Below are some ideas for "hope practices"—things that you can do to remember what brought you hope in the past (including the recent past), as well as suggestions for what you might do should you need a dose of hope in the future.

Keep a Hope Journal

You might begin one by reflecting on what brought you hope during this historically eventful time—when you were sheltering in place, before new vaccines were created and distributed, what brought you hope? What did you keep beside you for comfort—a special book, memories, a pet? Were those sources of hope different from the things that brought you hope in the past? What have you read about or seen others do that seemed like good ways to keep hope alive?

Create a "Hope Chest"

In the last century and earlier, a "hope chest" referred to a collection of linens and other household items collected by an unmarried woman who hoped to one day be wed. Clearly, it's time to update that notion; so as we move into the future, it might be a fruitful practice to create a different kind of "hope chest"—or at least a basket or box of hope, which hopefully will include *Have Hope*. You might start your own collection of hope quotations, or make a hope scrapbook filled with words and images that bring you hope. Having a collection of hope-filled resources for the days ahead could serve not only you, but also anyone else with whom you might want to share your hope quotations.

Collect Biographies and Other Works by Hope "Heroes"

Real-life examples of people who embody hope through their thoughts, words, and deeds can bring hope to nearly everyone. Whose example makes you feel hopeful that you can make it through any challenge? Whose life story makes you feel hopeful that you can achieve what you want to bring to the world? One place to start could be with the people who have offered us hope during our national season of sheltering-in-place—people like Stacey Abrams, whose dedication to voters' rights in Georgia led to two historic elections in that state, giving people around the country newfound hope; or like Amanda Gorman, whose poise and presence as the youngest poet ever to read at a US presidential inauguration gave us hope for the voices of the future. (And young Ms. Gorman wants to run for president in 2036!) Start a collection on your bookshelf of works by and about such "hope heroes."

Immerse Yourself in the Cycles of Nature

For many, spending time outdoors, where one can really experience the cycles of nature, is an inherently hopeful practice. By doing so, we are able to see how nature has rhythms of dormancy and growth—and that just when winter seems its coldest and meanest, the tiniest green shoots remind us that new growth and new life are just around the seasonal corner. *Have Hope* included mentions of the four seasons to remind us of how Mother Nature herself gives us hope each year, with the beginning of every Spring. Consider beginning a little nature altar in your home where you can be reminded of this—a small collection of seeds, seashells, dried fall leaves, and pinecones can help you to remember that any particular stage in life is part of a greater cycle.

Explore Faith, Prayer, and Meditation

For billions of people around the world, personal faith is the foundation for their sense of hope, strengthened by the practice of prayer. Others may not follow a traditional faith path but still define themselves as being spiritual, turning to practices which may be inspired by a particular religion but have since become more widely used—such as creating small altars for reflection in their home (see above). Still others find meaning in arenas completely outside of religion or spirituality. Yet for all of us, whether we define ourselves as religious, spiritual, or otherwise, hope can be found in secularized practices that include yoga, breathing exercises, meditation, and more. Simply sitting in silence for three to five minutes and focusing on a person, place, or thing that makes you feel hopeful can go a long way in shifting a negative perspective; add a prayer, affirmation, or blessing to that, and it becomes an even more powerful practice.

Support Your Vision by Taking Action

US founding father Benjamin Franklin once famously said, "He who lives upon hope will die fasting." At first glance, this seems like a negative commentary on hope, but pundits have explained this phrase as meaning that it is not enough just to hope—one must also take action to make what one hopes for happen! We all know that there are always steps we can take to support our hopes for our own lives, for our children's and grandchildren's lives, and for our world…even if those steps seem sometimes to be very small. But again, looking back at the unprecedented year of 2020, we see real evidence of how the actions of many supported the vision and hopes of all—we see how the work of dedicated scientists led to the creation of several efficacious vaccines; how millions of people protesting in our country and globally led to new individual and collective commitments to transform racism; and how the work of many tireless volunteers in 2020 led to a safe and secure election with record voter turn-out in the midst of a pandemic. Want to feel hope? Do something—anything—to support your vision, even if it's just writing a check for a cause you believe in.

Remember That You Are Creative

Some things that gave me hope during this unprecedented time were both exercising my own creativity and seeing the creativity of others. Indeed, during 2020, I took a couple of in-depth trainings to become a facilitator of two methodologies—Cosmic Smash Booking, a form of mixed-media art journaling, and SoulCollage®, in which one makes a personal deck of collaged cards in order to both express and understand conscious and unconscious movements in one's life. And of course, in 2020, I researched and began work on this book—*Have Hope*, the process of which proved to be such a blessing to me, sifting through these hope-filled entries throughout time, and I hope to you too.

For me, this last hope practice is perhaps the most important one—to remember that you are creative. This is not because following your creativity will lead to many blissful hours manifesting something that never existed before, which it will...but because remembering that you are creative will help you to know that you have the power to create hope through your thoughts, words, and actions. You can be—you are—a beacon of hope. At any given moment, you can pivot from a despairing thought to a hopeful one and help heal the world.

I leave you with this incredible poem by Kayleen Asbo, "The Ninth Symphony," which not only is an expression of her own creativity but which also exalts the creativity of the German composer and pianist Ludwig van Beethoven, and expresses so beautifully what happens when we make that choice to move from dark to light, from despair to hope.

The Ninth Symphony

It's possible
that the apocalyptic rumors and reports are right—
that these are the end times
and that the fire-ash falling from the sky
that covered everything for weeks last year
was only a prelude
to the larger conflagration to come.

It's conceivable
that the floods
and shootings
and suicides
and daily extinctions
will not wane,
but bleed their dark hues
into a shattering crescendo in the years that follow
leading us to total annihilation.

But the old ones knew
that relentless tragedy could also be the beginning
of transformation—
could become paint on the cave wall,
song in a scarred throat
the drumming heartbeat of a dance of lamentation
that would lead us to a deeper truth.

I think of that long scream of terror
that opens the last movement of Beethoven's
Ninth Symphony,
the cacophonous descent that signals the end of the world
and how the orchestra tries so valiantly to recapture the past
recapitulating one theme after another from the first
three movements.

How each time, the Greek Chorus of the orchestra says:

No.
This will not do.
We cannot go back to where we have already been.

And that moment—when all seems lost in utter chaos
and darkness—
how slowly,
tentatively,
ever so gently
emerging from the soft underbelly of the strings
is the simplest of tunes—
Childlike,
almost embarrassing
in its utter transparency and
open hearted
vulnerability

And how the goosebumps rise upon my neck
as the melody begins its sure ascent
Higher
Higher
Until it blazes with triumph,
blossoming into the Ode to Joy,
Shattering all notions of what a symphony should be
What a symphony could be.

I wonder if Beethoven,
gripped with liver disease and completely deaf
knew as he flailed his swollen hands
that his agony had opened the door to a new vision
for the entire human race.

I imagine how his sad eyes would open wide with wonder
If he could see his simple tune sung at Auschwitz,
as Chinese students faced tanks in Tiananmen Square,
if he could hear it sung at the fall of the Berlin Wall,
and see the choirs all across the world after 911
uniting the world into his lifelong dream:
a chorus of common humanity, resounding with love.

Let us sing with all we have in us
no matter what storms rage all around,
and know this in our bones:
If a deaf and dying man
(who believed his whole life was a failure)
could give birth to such miraculous starshine as this,
surely,
surely,
there is still hope
for us all.

—Kayleen Asbo, "The Ninth Symphony"

ACKNOWLEDGMENTS

I first want to acknowledge the wisdom and inspiration of all the people whose names appear in *Have Hope*; they span different centuries and continents, races and genders, but share the commonality of using their gifts and talents in service of advancing humankind in some fashion. To them, I am grateful.

I also want to thank Phil Cousineau for the blessing of his foreword, and for the gifts of inspiration that he has provided me repeatedly as a teacher, colleague, and friend.

And how wonderful it is to acknowledge again Brenda Knight and her team at Mango Publishing; Brenda has been the common denominator of all nine of my books, whose publication dates now span almost a quarter-century. I am so delighted to also deliver *Have Hope* under her auspices after lo these many years!

As always, deep gratitude to my family—my husband Scott and my daughter Chloe—for their patience and understanding as I was putting this book together, and for the hope they give me on a daily basis. Thanks, too, to my congregation at Unity Spiritual Center of San Francisco, whose presence in my life has been a blessing.

Above all, I give gratitude to my Creator and the words that have meant so much to me throughout the journey of my life, found in Jeremiah 29:11: " 'For I know the plans I have for you,' declares the Lord, 'plans to prosper you and not to harm you, plans to give you hope and a future.' "

I give deepest thanks for that hope, which has guided not only my past and present, but also will continue to shape my future.

About the Author

The Reverend Maggie Oman Shannon, MA, is an ordained Unity minister, spiritual director, workshop and retreat facilitator, and author of eight previous books: *Prayers for Healing; The Way We Pray: Prayer Practices from Around the World; A String and a Prayer: How to Make and Use Prayer Beads* (coauthor); *One God, Shared Hope; Prayers for Hope and Comfort; Crafting Calm: Projects and Practices for Creativity and Contemplation; Crafting Gratitude: Creating and Celebrating Our Blessings with Hands and Heart;* and *Crafting Love: Sharing Our Hearts through the Work of Our Hands.*

The former editor of three national magazines, including the *Saturday Evening Post*, Oman Shannon also served as Director of Marketing for the Institute of Noetic Sciences. Her work has been featured in periodicals ranging from the *San Francisco Chronicle* to *Spirituality and Health* magazine. She has taught workshops at venues including California Pacific Medical Center's Institute for Health and Healing and Chautauqua Institution in Chautauqua, New York. A graduate of Smith College, Oman Shannon also holds a master of arts degree in Culture and Spirituality from Holy Names University. A 2010 graduate of Manhattan's One Spirit Interfaith Seminary, she was ordained as a Unity minister in 2014. Oman Shannon is the senior minister of Unity Spiritual

Center of San Francisco and has served as its spiritual leader since 2010.

Creativity as a spiritual practice is her passion, and other pursuits include having been the host of a weekly, hour-long radio show called "Creative Spirit" for three years; becoming certified as an Intentional Creativity teacher in 2018, and as a SoulCollage® facilitator and Cosmic Smash Book facilitator in 2020; and pursuing her own creative outlets. She lives in San Francisco with her husband and soon-to-be college-bound daughter. You can learn more about her at www.maggieomanshannon.com.